THE DIGITAL DIVIDE

THE DIGITAL DIVIDE

STANDING AT THE INTERSECTION OF RACE & TECHNOLOGY

Raneta Lawson Mack

PROFESSOR, CREIGHTON UNIVERSITY
SCHOOL OF LAW

CAROLINA ACADEMIC PRESS
Durham, North Carolina

ISBN 0-89089-641-0
LCCN 2001092053

CAROLINA ACADEMIC PRESS
700 Kent Street
Durham, North Carolina 27701
Telephone (919) 489-7486
Fax (919)493-5668
www.cap-press.com

Printed in the United States of America

For my daughter Kandace,
you have blessed my life

Contents

Preface

Divides and Intersections. At first glance, these concepts seem diametrically opposed and mutually exclusive. Yet, if one carefully examines what is currently described as the "digital divide" or the "technology gap" between the haves and have nots, it will quickly become apparent that this divide is not of recent origin and is, in fact, a proxy for the myriad societal divisions that have resulted from the historical legacy of racism in America. This current "divide" thus represents an intersection of the legacy of racism and the promise of technology. The past and the present are colliding and dividing, and the divisions are palpable. We see it in low-income schools where technology education is not part of the curriculum because school systems cannot afford to purchase updated textbooks, much less computer technology. We see it in the homes of people in underserved communities where computer technology is not valued because it is not considered relevant or because economic circumstances simply do not permit expenditures for such "luxury" items. We will begin to see it in the workplace where the digital economy will compel employers to give preferential hiring treatment to those who have technology skills or training, while eliminating jobs that do not require such competencies.

As we embark upon a new century, how we address the divisions created by the technology gap will rest in large part upon our understanding of how the legacy of racism has set the stage for the current division that threatens to leave behind millions of Americans who are unprepared and, in some cases, unwilling to become part of the digital revolution. At the same time, however, the intersection of race and technology is also a crossroads of opportunity. At this crossroads, the haves can choose to increase the opportunity for partici-

xi

pation of the have nots by ensuring that technology resources and education are widely available and relevant. The have-nots can choose to become active participants in the digital revolution by educating themselves about the ever increasing opportunities for full participation in the new economy.

This book is an exploration of the divisions that beset us and the corresponding choices that confront us as we seek to ensure that no person is left behind. I hope it can serve as an informational resource for those who share the concern of narrowing the divide and expanding opportunities for equal participation in the digital economy.

I would like to thank Dean Patrick Borchers and the Creighton University School of Law for providing me with funding and support for the research and writing of this book. I am also grateful to my husband John and my daughter Kandace for their love, encouragement and support throughout the drafting process.

Introduction

This book is a call to arms. It is a rallying cry for everyone, regardless of race or economic circumstances, to immediately arm themselves with the necessary technological knowledge and skills to compete in the rapidly expanding digital economy. As those who follow technology trends and predictions know, barely a week goes by without mention of the widening "digital divide." This term has become the political and sociological catch-phrase to describe the growing disparity between the "haves" and the "have-nots" in the current digital revolution. Although the terms "haves" and "have-nots" encompass a variety of racial, ethnic and socioeconomic groups, the largest and most noteworthy differential is developing between blacks and whites, two groups that have been divided on myriad bases throughout the course of history. Thus, in many respects, it is as if this historical divide is simply repeating itself on the technology landscape. However, without underestimating the impact of previous divisions between the races, the digital divide has perhaps the greatest potential to doom the "have-nots" to the status of permanent underclass. Before discussing the disadvantages that will almost certainly flow from being left behind in the technology race, it is important to examine the most recent statistics concerning telephone, computer and Internet access and usage. This information offers insight into how current technology is penetrating target markets and reveals where disparities in access and usage are most pervasive. The statistics are appalling, yet not very surprising.

In *Falling Through the Net II*, the National Telecommunications and Information Administration (NTIA) published the results of its detailed examination of technology access and usage in the United States. At the outset, the report confirmed the importance of computers and Internet technology in today's society by observing that, "[t]he Internet is a nascent, rapidly diffusing technology that promises to become the economic underpinning for all the successful countries in the new global economy." The NTIA report further explained that "understanding who is connected to the Net, and how it is being used, is critical to the development of sound policies in this area." The study examined three areas of technology access and usage—telephones, personal computers and the Internet—and determined that, with respect to telephones, approximately 94% of the people in America own a telephone set at home. Yet, even with what amounts to nearly universal access to telephones, there is still a marked disparity when the ownership numbers are broken down by demographics. Specifically, those who are low-income, minority, less-educated or single parents are less likely to have a telephone at home. Although telephones are not new technology, they are the most frequently used means to access the Internet from home. Therefore, an examination of telephone ownership is important because it identifies those households that have established the prerequisite to Internet access.

The study also determined that although household rates of personal computer ownership and Internet access have dramatically increased since 1994 for all demographic groups, some areas of the digital divide have nevertheless widened. For instance, black households are far less likely than white households to own personal computers and have Internet access.[1] Indeed, during the four year period between 1994 and 1998, the computer ownership gap between white and black households grew from a 16.8% difference to a 23.4% difference. In terms of Internet access, the gap widened similarly from 13.5% to 18.6% during that same period. The study summarized all of the findings by stating that while "all Americans are becoming increasingly connected... certain groups are growing far more rapidly [which] means that the "haves" have only become more informa-

---

1. According to the NTIA report, whites are twice as likely to own computers and have access to the Internet than blacks. The percentages for whites owning computers and accessing the Internet are 46.6% and 29.8% respectively, while black ownership and access is 23.2% and 11.2% respectively.

tion-rich in 1998 while the "have-nots" are lagging even further behind." In terms of policy implications, the NTIA report advised that efforts to resolve the digital divide should continue to focus primarily upon low-income, minority and young populations because these groups "could most use electronic services to find jobs, housing and other services."

This compelling observation highlights one of the bitter ironies of the digital divide. That is, those groups that could most benefit from the informational resources and convenience afforded by computers and Internet access are precisely the groups that are lagging behind. This is indeed an unfortunate consequence because as technology continues to permeate more and more of our daily existence, knowledge and capabilities in this area may no longer be a matter of curiosity and optional convenience, but may become a necessary tool for survival. For example, consider some of the more recent technological advances.

- By the end of the year 2000, General Motors (GM) plans to offer voice activated Internet access in one of its vehicles. GM predicts that within five years, in-car services such as Internet access could generate revenues of four to six billion dollars annually. GM also plans to make it easier for consumers to purchase automobiles online and equip them with a variety of on-board services via satellite.

- In September 1999, the United Network for Organ Sharing unveiled Transplant Living, an Internet program that provides transplant patients with detailed information on the organ transplant process. Among other things, the program will enable transplant patients to quickly locate health care centers that provide organs. United Network also plans to develop UNET, a secure Internet program to exchange information on patients and potential donors.

- In March 2000, Arizona Democrats held their state presidential primary online. Although there were a number of security and authentication glitches, the major challenge to online voting was a lawsuit filed by an organization known as Voting Integrity Project. The group argued unsuccessfully that voting online would effectively disenfranchise the state's minority population and, in fact, it almost did. To alleviate this concern, party leaders offered absentee ballot voting to allow users without computers to vote from home. Perhaps not surprisingly, many more minority voters used the absentee ballots, while whites used their personal computers to vote from home.

* Internet "people auctions" now allow job seekers to sell their skills to the highest online bidder. This idea adds a new wrinkle to the online job recruiting process, where employers are projected to spend as much as $1.7 billion dollars by the year 2003 searching for employees.

* And finally, how would you like to make a back-up copy of your life? Scientists are currently researching ways to join mind and memory chips. If successful, this technology could potentially be used to recreate a person's life just as he or she experienced it. This extraordinary use of memory chip technology, known as the "Soul Catcher," is both intriguing and alarming. As everyone has probably felt at one time or another, there are some life events that are best forgotten. How frustrating it might be to have those same memories indelibly imprinted on a memory chip!

These are but a few examples of the numerous ways in which technology is rapidly becoming intertwined in our lives, for better or worse. As statistics clearly demonstrate, most Americans are embracing these changes and many are reveling in the added convenience and efficiency these innovations provide. For some segments of the population, however, adapting to meet the demands of the technology revolution is not even a remote consideration. Indeed, to some of these individuals, computers and the Internet are viewed as an unnecessary luxury at best, and a potential intrusion into personal privacy at worst. This intransigent group of "have-nots" is unlikely to be persuaded to adopt technology no matter how many free or reduced price computers are provided. These individuals actively reject technology in their lives and will be relegated to the perimeter of our information technology driven society .

On the other hand, there is another group of "have-nots" who could be persuaded to explore and eventually embrace technology if the costs and benefits of adoption are clearly articulated in terms that illustrate the severe long-term personal and professional consequences of ignoring the digital revolution. This is perhaps the most overlooked aspect of current strategies to narrow the digital divide. As with many social issues that disproportionately impact minority groups, there is a constant dialogue between politicians and academics decrying the fact that there is an ever widening technology gap. But there is very little discussion *between* these groups and the affected segments of the population about the real consequences of permitting these divisions to persist.

In other words, why is it important for minority children to attend science and technology summer camps instead of or in addition to the traditional summer sports camps? Why is it important that technology become a required part of inner city school curriculums as early as first or second grade? Why is it equally important for the parents of children in these schools to make a similar commitment to explore technology and make every effort to bring it into the home? Why is it important to not only establish technology centers in urban areas, but to perhaps make the receipt of certain government benefits dependent upon taking basic computer skills courses?

The answer is, in part, because we are rapidly approaching what might be considered a digital fork in the road where the "haves" and "have nots" will be so widely separated in terms of information technology skills that there will be no hope of ever reuniting these divergent paths. Quite simply, to be left behind in the digital age is to be unemployed, information-deprived and subject to a continual "technology tax" on goods and services that are more expensive to consumers who don't utilize Internet technology. These are significant disadvantages, which are already becoming reality. For example, a number of employers now require potential employees to demonstrate some familiarity with computer technology even though their jobs may not require them to interact with computers on a daily basis. Thus, job applicants are weeded out in the initial phases of the recruitment process if they cannot demonstrate a minimal level of computer competency. Additionally, employment advertisements for all types of occupations are increasingly finding a home on the Internet. Job seekers who are adept at the online job search process will undoubtedly have a considerable advantage over those who continue to search by traditional means.

Furthermore, as technology becomes more ingrained in our culture, the means of distributing information will be driven by the electronic and wireless markets. Today, in addition to the traditional media outlets, many people receive news and information through a variety of electronic sources. With the wireless technology revolution upon us, it will not be uncommon for people to regularly carry their news and information sources with them, receiving periodic updates throughout the day. Less expensive means of communicating will also be technology based. We have already witnessed the tremendous effect of e-mail as a modern communication device. E-mail users appreciate and frequently take advantage of the instantaneous and low cost nature of this communication tool as evidenced by the fact that the use of e-mail easily outpaces all other aspects of Internet use. Now, with the possibility of voice over the Internet, long distance voice communications are also making inroads into Internet technology.

Retail establishments, financial institutions and health care providers are also moving toward an Internet model to make their services accessible to customers 24 hours a day. As an extra incentive, some Internet merchants offer reduced rates or additional services to customers who choose to conduct business on the Internet. Because web sites typically aren't as costly to maintain as brick and mortar establishments, some merchants are willing to pass these savings on to Internet consumers.

These examples demonstrate that the momentum is clearly in the direction of more technology, not less. Therefore, an obvious question arises: why *wouldn't* everyone want to be a part of the digital revolution? The answer is multi-faceted.

First, many cite cost as a factor in their decision not to purchase a computer or obtain Internet access. Yet, today, with the price of computers dropping to an all-time low, the question is no longer who *can* afford technology, but who *can't*. Of course, this is not to suggest that there aren't still some segments of the population whose economic circumstances are so severe that the purchase of a computer is com-

pletely outside of their financial reach. However, due to dramatic re-
ductions in the price of computer technology, that group is shrinking
to the point that it can hardly be said that cost presents the barrier to
entry that it once did. A similar observation may be made with respect
to trends in Internet service. Although prices vary, the average cost of
an unlimited access plan can range from $20–$25 a month. In addition, there are a number of companies now offering free Internet access. In most cases, consumers pay no fee to access the Internet, but
must agree to view targeted advertisements as they use the service. For
some, this might be considered a minor annoyance when weighed
against the access to information gained by using the Internet.

Another argument often advanced as an explanation for not acquiring technology is that, to some, computers and the Internet have
very little usefulness in their daily lifestyles. Technology just doesn't
fit or seem relevant. Perhaps these individuals prefer to get their
news from other formal or informal sources, or they prefer to engage
in face-to-face communication, or they would rather shop locally for
goods and services. There is just no *perceived* place for computer
technology in their lives. In these circumstances, often what is required is exposure and education.

Other arguments against technology adoption relate to misperceptions about the difficulty of learning basic skills. Based upon no experience or a previous negative experience, many perceive computers as
complicated to understand and difficult to maintain. They believe it is
unlikely that these "gadgets" would make life easier and would only
serve to make things more confusing and, thus, inefficient. Finally, the
perceived lack of privacy is a significant cause of concern for many as
frequent news stories reveal how technology may be manipulated to
intrude into the personal privacy of unsuspecting individuals. But can
these arguments against technology justify allowing the digital divide
to persist? Consider this tale of two towns.

In an article entitled, *A Small Town Reveals America's Digital Divide,* Marcia Stepanek describes how the technology gap is impact-
ing a community on the edge of rural Appalachia.[2] The article is

---

2. Marcia Stepanek, *A Small Town Reveals America's Digital Divide* BusinessWeek Online (October 4, 1999).

brief, but few have written as poignantly and insightfully about the realities of the digital divide. Stepanek describes the relatively prosperous town of Blacksburg, Virginia, where Virginia Polytechnic Institute and State University sponsored the creation of Blacksburg Electronic Village (BEV) to bring Internet access to homes in the area. Although most of Blacksburg is now wired and, indeed, Blacksburg is the most wired town in the nation, the surrounding areas lag far behind in access to technology. The contrasts are staggering. For instance, Lori Atwater, a thirty-nine year old single mom in Blacksburg, changed her life dramatically by utilizing the resources provided by the BEV Internet access program. After working for 10 years as a meter maid at $6 an hour, Atwater decided to use her son's computer and the inexpensive BEV.net Internet connection to teach herself how to design web pages. After mastering the technology, Atwater quit her job to become president of Lori Atwater Enterprises, a web design company where she earns three times her previous salary as a meter maid.

In contrast, just outside of Blacksburg in the town of Christiansburg, nearly one-third of the adults do not have high school diplomas and Internet connections are few. Although the town hoped to benefit from the same BEV project that brought low cost Internet access to Blacksburg, that assistance has not materialized. Many of the residents cannot afford computers or Internet access and parents worry that their children are being left behind because the schools do not yet have computer training as part of their curriculum. To make matters worse, even the few technology resources available in Christiansburg sit gathering dust because there is no one to provide training on the equipment and many of the residents simply lack interest in the technology. Stepanek sums up the lesson from this experience in this way: "Making equipment and Net connections available isn't enough. The Internet haves must find a way to introduce folks to the technology and then to make access meaningful to those without. It's the difference between giving people a book and teaching them how to read."[3]

---

3. *Id.*

The harsh realities of the Blacksburg experience raise the fundamental question of whether the technology gap between the haves and have nots can ever be narrowed or closed, or is it an inevitable result of a society in which information is treated as a market commodity? William F. Birdsall, in an article examining the Canadian digital divide, concluded that because of the "ideology of information technology" and the "dual social structure" in both the United States and Canada, the "policy debate in time will not be over how to eliminate the digital divide but only how large or small it should be."[4] According to Birdsall, the ideology of information technology began to emerge in the United States in the 1970s. The premise of this ideology is that:

> information technology is inevitably driving the shift from an industrial society to an information society. The raw material or basic commodity of this society's knowledge-based economy is information. In the knowledge-based economy only the marketplace should determine which goods and services are produced and how they are generated; there are no public goods.[5]

In this model, government's role is to promote a competitive market through deregulation and privatization rather than ensuring equality of access to goods and services. Birdsall posits that both the United States and Canada are liberal welfare states, where the work ethic prevails and welfare entitlements are distributed only to those who meet strict criteria. For those who do not meet the criteria, the government allows the market to provide and distribute benefits. This creates a dual social benefit structure where most attain benefits through the market and a few receive them from the government with the expectation that they will eventually attain them from the market as well. The choice to treat information as a market commodity creates a digital divide in the sense that, just as any other good, those who are able to attain information through the market will do so, while those who can't will simply have to rely upon either

---

4. William F. Birdsall, *The Digital Divide in the Liberal State: A Canadian Perspective* First Monday(5) (2000).
5. *Id.*

limited government assistance or the good will of private enterprise. Given these circumstances, Birdsall argues that one possibility for eliminating the digital divide rests upon "recognizing that technology is a social construct and that access in the information society cannot be left to the market alone."[6]

Although Birdsall offers a persuasive analysis of how the digital divide is an inevitable result of social welfare policy in certain countries, his analysis perhaps underestimates the degree to which the market may act in its self interest to increase consumer access to technology. To the degree that the market relies upon maximizing customer base for profitability, it cannot wait indefinitely for the government bureaucratic engine to generate programs that distribute benefits to the "have-nots." Thus, private enterprise may act on its own, investing in underserved communities and ultimately investing in its own future. Consider, for example, Fleet Bank's recent announcement that it is launching one of the "most comprehensive community economic development initiatives in the nation to help close the technology gap and create greater access to financial services and the Internet for individuals and businesses in low-and moderate-income communities."[7] Fleet's plan is to introduce a program called CommunityLink, which will provide community based content, in-home training and computers to lower income people. Importantly, Fleet's plan recognizes that access to technology is not enough and "[has] identified comfort of use and relevancy of content as crucial components to sustained usage and creation of wealth."[8] Although it is obvious that Fleet hopes to build long-term and profitable customer relationships through this program, it is also "functioning as a catalyst for change in community economic redevelopment."[9] Fleet's multi-focused approach to alleviating the hardships imposed by the digital divide in one community is commendable for its recognition that the problem is not merely one of access. Increasing public awareness about the variety of factors that

6. *Id.*
7. Beth Cox, *Crossing the Great Digital Divide* ECommerce Guide (December 12, 2000).
8. *Id.*
9. *Id.*

contribute to the digital divide helps turn the focus toward finding creative solutions rather than blaming the "have-nots."

In furtherance of that goal, this book will discuss three separate although interrelated topics. In the first section, "Exploring the Reasons," the book will revisit the historical bases for the economic and educational differences that divide racial groups in the United States. The section will discuss how a tragic history of legally enforced divisions along racial lines in the areas of economics and education has contributed to a similar divide in the area of technology. This section will also explore how fears related to technology may also be rooted in earlier practices that manipulated science and technology to the detriment of black Americans.

Part II, "The Impact of the Digital Divide," will provide a fairly comprehensive overview of how technology has made inroads into everyday life, making it easier to complete commonplace tasks such as shopping and banking more conveniently and efficiently. This section also reveals how computer technology is increasingly becoming the standard way of interacting and doing business and explains why those who are unfamiliar with technology run an extremely high risk of being left behind and becoming part of a permanent virtual underclass.

Finally, Part III, "Solutions to Close the Gap," will examine some options to reduce or eliminate the digital divide. Ideas ranging from community access centers to corporate partnerships with schools will be explored. This section concludes that while all of these efforts are admirable, in the end, none will be successful unless those promoting them are able to overcome the wall of suspicion and lack of interest that often prevents minority communities from taking full advantage of these opportunities.

PART I

EXPLORING THE
REASONS

Chapter 1

Fear of Science and Technology

One of the more recent Internet rumors to make the virtual rounds involves the slogan "NO FEAR." For several years the term "NO FEAR" has been the catch phrase of a company that specializes in trendy sports apparel. However, it seems that David Duke, a proponent of the rights of white people and one-time candidate for governor in Louisiana, is now starting a new white-rights group called No Fear, which, according to Duke, is an acronym for National Organization For European American Rights.[1] While these facts probably establish the basis for a trademark infringement lawsuit, interestingly enough, they also provided the impetus for yet another race-related urban legend that circulated quickly across the Internet via e-mail.

The forwarded e-mail read, in part:

> To make a long story short, David Duke, former grand wizard for the KKK, was in town to speak at a shopping mall. David Duke is the head of a group calling itself NO FEAR; it stands for: "National Organization For European-American Rights."

> All this time I thought No Fear was just something young white people placed onto their vehicles, meaning they fear nothing because of their youth. How wrong I was, so please pass this on so that more of our people know what No Fear really means.

---

1. The company No Fear, Inc. has sued Duke for trademark infringement.

3

Closer examination of the content of this e-mail reveals that the author has taken the basic facts of the "No Fear" dispute and merged them in such a fashion that readers are led to believe that the No Fear company and David Duke's organization are one and the same. Moreover, several race-based ideas are conveyed by this e-mail, both implicitly and explicitly. First, the author speaks of the term No Fear as if it is exclusively associated with young white people. In fact, there is no evidence that the company markets solely to white youth and No Fear has expressly disavowed any such marketing strategy.[2] Second, the e-mail, by its use of the term "our people," suggests that it was authored by a person of color with the intent that it be passed on to other people of color as a warning to avoid anything associated with No Fear. Although the company No Fear stepped in and attempted to quash this rumor shortly after it surfaced, chances are, given the relative speed of e-mail communications and the willingness by some to believe rumors of this nature, this urban legend will have some degree of staying power.

Race-related urban legends are not a recent phenomenon. What is new, however, is that e-mail and the Internet are being used to transmit them to a much wider audience; an audience that is, for a variety of reasons, particularly susceptible to belief in rumor and conspiracy. The Internet is thus serving as a medium to perpetuate longstanding fears and instill new ones. Other race-related urban legends that have enjoyed a long shelf life on the Internet include, the warning that black voting rights will expire in 2007, the idea that social security numbers are somehow encoded to reveal the race of the owner, a story that the Statue of Liberty was intended as a tribute to black slaves, and the ubiquitous and enduring tale of how Tommy Hilfiger made racist statements on the Oprah show.[3] These mes-

---

2. No Fear Inc. issued a press release which stated, in part:
    No Fear is a sports company founded a decade ago with the intent of instilling positive messages of self-esteem through the medium of competitive sport, and inspiring all people to perform to their potential.
3. So as not to participate in the perpetuation of these urban legends, I should note that each of them has been thoroughly or partially debunked. The Voting Rights Act of 1965 is indeed due to expire and come up for re-

sages, at least when they are transmitted via e-mail, tend to follow a specific formula. For example, the messages are usually forwarded by a well-meaning relative or friend and arrive as a warning or alert to the recipient. The text of the message typically reveals stories of shocking discrimination or recently discovered conspiracies against minorities and may even claim to have been "verified" by "legitimate" sources. The message concludes by imploring the recipient to forward the message to as many people as possible. In most cases, it is either stated explicitly or implied by the context of the message that it should be sent immediately to other black people.

In these instances, the Internet is being used as a means for quickly transmitting information that would otherwise be shared orally, if at all. The fact that the Internet provides access to a global audience makes it difficult to locate the "root" of these urban legends, thereby making the debunking process much more problematic. One question that might be raised at this point is why do those who apparently embrace or at least utilize Internet and e-mail technology choose to use it in such a fashion? That is, what compels people to forward such race-based misinformation when a few minutes of additional research would reveal that the majority of these urban legends cannot be substantiated and are patently false? Additionally, and perhaps more important, can the virtual exchange of this type of information by those in minority communities who

---

newal in 2007, but according to the Department of Justice, the basic right to vote, which is guaranteed by the Fifteenth Amendment, is permanent and will not expire with the Voting Rights Act. The social security number urban legend warned that the fifth number on social security cards of minority citizens is always even and employers are beginning to use this code as a basis for discriminating against minority job applicants. In fact, statistically, it is more likely that the fifth number on *anyone's* social security card will be an odd number given the method used by the Social Security Administration to assign the numbers. The Statue of Liberty rumor has only been partially debunked and research continues into whether the statue may have some relationship to the abolitionist movement. However, historical documents tend to suggest that the statue was not intended solely as a tribute to black slaves. Finally, Tommy Hilfiger has consistently denied the racist statements attributed to him on the Oprah show and, indeed, he has never appeared on the show at all.

have developed some technological savvy provide insight (albeit ironic) into why others in those same communities might be reluctant to jump on the technological bandwagon? This chapter will explore those questions and demonstrate how legitimate historically-based fears concerning science and technology play a considerable role in the modern day reluctance of minority communities to fully take advantage of the digital revolution.

The Legacy of Slavery

It can hardly be disputed that the atrocities of slavery have left an indelible mark on the collective psyche of blacks in America. No other group of Americans shares a similar history of being subjected to utter degradation and humiliation both during and after the forced immigration of Africans to America as slave labor. This chapter does not propose to explore the history of black slavery in America. There are ample texts available that provide exhaustive analyses of this horrific chapter in American history. But, what this chapter will explore are some lingering beliefs and attitudes that likely trace their roots back to slavery and the post-slavery Jim Crow era and, as a consequence, directly impact the current thinking of black Americans about "advances" in technology.

In his book, *Shadows of Race and Class*, Raymond Franklin poses the question: Was the system of slavery benign or evil? This question is profoundly important because, as Franklin observes, it has relevance to current perceptions and judgments of and by contemporary blacks.[4] According to Franklin, there is no precise answer to this question and scholars occasionally "reconstruct history in their endeavors to cope with present and often unanticipated events."[5] More specifically, if slavery was indeed a benign system then theoretically, there should be no lingering damage to black Americans, psychic or otherwise. Therefore, to the extent that blacks today have failed to pull themselves up by their bootstraps, then it must be largely a result of

---

4. Raymond S. Franklin, Shadows of Race and Class 23 (1991).
5. *Id.*

their individual character weaknesses.[6] In contrast, however, if slavery was as evil and harmful to blacks as is widely believed, then lingering debilities render blacks as a group inherently incapable of caring for themselves and forever cast them in the role of "white man's burden." Thus, while the reasons may differ, all roads lead to perceptions of inferiority and dependency.

No matter how extensively scholars debate the nature and consequences of slavery, very few can dispute the fact that slavery was a social holocaust that brutally separated blacks from their homeland and resulted in a "form of raw economic exploitation in the American context not comparable to that experienced by other exploited immigrant groups."[7] It is also scarcely debatable that each side in this historic tragedy has been left with profound and lingering perceptions of the other. For many whites, slavery, whether benign or evil, was undoubtedly justified because blacks were lazy, unintelligent, uneducable, and in constant need of supervision lest they give in to their "natural" tendencies for crime and wanton sexuality. For blacks, the white slavemaster was not to be trusted. With the stroke of a pen, he could separate families or send them to their deaths. Everyday life was a struggle for mental and physical survival in the face of insurmountable odds. Long ago, Frederick Douglass passionately described the daily travails of slave life. He wrote:

> The motto which I adopted when I started from slavery was this—"Trust no man!" I saw in every white man an enemy; and in almost every colored cause for distrust. It was a most painful situation; and, to understand it, one must need to experience it or imagine himself in similar circumstances. Let him be a fugitive slave in a strange land—a land given up to be the hunting-ground for slaveholders—whose inhabitants are legalized kidnappers—where he is every moment subjected to the terrible liability of being seized upon by his fellowmen, as the hideous crocodile seizes upon prey!—I say let

6. The notion of a "benign" system suggests that the institution of slavery was the most compassionate and efficient means to educate and train the masses of Africans in America.

7. Franklin, SHADOWS, at 25.

him place himself in my situation—without home or friends—without money or credit—wanting shelter, and no one to give it—wanting bread, and no money to buy it,—and at the same time let him feel he is pursued by merciless menhunters, and in total darkness as to what to do, where to go and where to stay....I say, let him be placed in this most trying situation...then and not till then, will he fully appreciate the hardships of, and know how to sympathize with the toil-worn and whip-scarred fugitive slave.[8]

Although slavery is no longer lawfully practiced in the United States, attitudes that find their roots in the inhumanity of slavery persist. As mentioned above, many whites continue to view blacks through a dehumanizing prism that casts them in the role of criminals, sexual predators and societal leeches. Correspondingly, many blacks continue to view whites through a prism of mistrust, believing that somehow whites are perpetually conspiring to deprive them of their liberty and bodily integrity. These dueling perceptions no longer revolve around the institution of slavery and discover new territories to invade with each successive generation. In the modern age, these negative, historically based perceptions have taken root in the areas of science and technology. Throughout history, whites have used science, research and technology to continue their subjugation of blacks. Blacks, in turn, have learned to fear and mistrust scientific and technological developments, believing that such advancements are easily manipulated to suit the purposes of the dominant society. One of the first areas of science to be used in a manner that mirrored and arguably gave validity to the dominant society's negative perceptions about minorities was the "science" of measuring intelligence, more commonly known as IQ testing.

The Pseudoscience of IQ Testing

Speculation concerning the genetic basis of IQ differences traces its roots back at least one thousand years. At that time, people of Eu-

---

8. FREDERICK DOUGLASS, NARRATIVE OF THE LIFE OF FREDERICK DOUGLASS, AN AMERICAN SLAVE (1968).

ropean descent widely believed that Africans were intellectually inferior and sought ways to validate those beliefs with science in order to
further justify the continued oppression of an entire race of people.[9]
Unfortunately, those patently racist efforts have been largely successful as over the years the notion of IQ difference inevitably raises the
specters of race and class. Elaine Mensh and Harry Mensh, in their
book, *The IQ Mythology*, observe that race and class are inextricably
intertwined with IQ testing and further explain that:

> To say somebody has a "high IQ" or "low IQ" is, as everyone
> knows, to pass judgment on whether a person is "smart" or
> "dumb." If such judgments were made about individuals as
> individuals, they would be damaging enough. But—be-
> cause of the correspondence of IQ scores to race and
> class—they are not made simply about individuals as indi-
> viduals. To say someone has a low IQ is, as a rule, to cast as-
> persions on that person in a racial and/or class sense.[10]

Historically, IQ testing is rooted in the pseudoscience of craniometrics, the measurement of human skulls and brain sizes as a
means of extrapolating about an individual's relative position in society. Those who practiced craniometry during the time of slavery
used it to demonstrate that black slaves, by virtue of their brain sizes,
were biologically inferior to whites and therefore well suited to their
roles as servants to the biologically superior race. As might be expected given what is now known about the dubious connection between brain size and intelligence, craniometric "proof" of biological
inferiority was often falsified to correspond with expected and desired results and scientific logic was ignored. Indeed, as Mensh &
Mensh point out, "if brain size correlated with intelligence, some an-
imals would be smarter than human beings."[11] Nevertheless, these

---

9. It did not matter, of course, that the definition of "intelligence" was
based largely on a white European view of intelligence and applied to a
group whose cultural norms and values were dramatically different from
that ethnocentric view.

10. ELAINE MENSH & HARRY MENSH, THE IQ MYTHOLOGY: CLASS,
RACE, GENDER AND INEQUALITY 1 (1991).

11. *Id.* at 14.

pseudoscientific craniometric findings cemented the fundamental belief that mental acuity could be quantified and, thereafter, the race was on to develop a sound "scientific" way to justify subjugation of a race of people in the post-slavery era.

Not long after craniometrics was discredited as a means for measuring intelligence and it was generally acknowledged that brain size bears very little correlation to intelligence, French psychologist, Alfred Binet developed an intelligence scale that purportedly measured the education potential of mentally handicapped students. Binet's intelligence scales make him one of the most widely known and controversial characters in the history of IQ testing. While Binet maintained that his initial tests were designed to "discover" students who needed special education, many now believe that these tests were merely a subterfuge designed to confirm preconceived notions that the tested children were less intelligent. In fact, as Mensh & Mensh describe, Binet's race and class biases were readily apparent. For instance, when exploring reasons for the children's failure to achieve in the classroom setting, Binet neglected to consider that school conditions might be the reason for such poor performance. Instead, Binet's test "scientifically shifted the onus for school performance from school officials to school children."[12] Additionally, once the children were determined by Binet's intelligence scales to be in need of "special education" Binet concluded that they should be subjected to "lessons of will, of attention and discipline."[13] This non-academic solution for academic difficulties suggests that Binet believed the children ineducable and simply in need of basic discipline so as not to become disruptive influences on others around them. Apparently buoyed by his successful categorization of these "special education" children, Binet further speculated that his intelligence tests could be used to formulate the ideal city, "where everyone could work according to his known aptitudes."[14] Of course, it is understood that "ideal" means one's known aptitude would likely be a predetermined result validated by Binet's biased testing process. Binet's ideal city would there-

---

12. *Id.* at 21.
13. *Id.*
14. *Id.* at 23.

fore be a mere perpetuation of the social and racial stratification that already existed in the less than ideal world.

Although Binet's testing procedure was purported to have a more scientific basis than craniometry, upon closer examination, it is clear that much like the pseudoscience of craniometry, Binet's tests were formulated in a flawed, self-fulfilling fashion. While the tests appeared to objectively measure intelligence, in fact, initial versions of Binet's tests were correlated to school performance. Binet gave the tests to groups of school children and their scores were measured against their teachers' rating of classroom performance. Then, "items were added or deleted to bring about the closest correspondence between test performance and educational age norms."[15] Thus, students' success or failure on the tests depended largely on whether they were already doing well or poorly in school. Essentially then, the tests were keyed to a specific standard of school success that permitted no way to objectively validate the results.[16]

After the development of Binet's tests, the history of IQ testing took on more overtly racist overtones. At each juncture, test results continued to purportedly "verify" the intellectual inferiority of minority groups and simultaneously confirm the intellectual superiority of the white race. Moreover, many, not content to tolerate brushing elbows with the mentally inferior, took these "scientific" results one step further by advocating that those of inferior intelligence not only be separated from others in society, but that they be sterilized so as not to reproduce others of lesser intelligence.[17]

---

15. *Id.* at 42.

16. Binet nevertheless created the illusion of validity by introducing mystifying terminology such as "mental age" and arbitrary standards. *Id.* at 43.

17. The United States Supreme Court even ventured into the controversial call for forced sterilization of those deemed to be mentally inferior. In Buck v. Bell, Mr. Justice Oliver Wendell Holmes declared that:

> We have seen more than once that the public welfare may call upon the best citizens for their lives. It would be strange if it could not call upon those who already sap the strength of the State for these lesser sacrifices... in order to prevent our being swamped by incompetence. It is better for all the world, if instead of waiting to execute

In reality, what these tests did was provide a pseudoscientific rationale to act upon fundamental beliefs that were already pervasive in society. They lent credence to the notion that those who were in the elite classes were there because they were biologically superior and, of course, those at the bottom were there because they were biologically inferior. These pseudoscientific rationales not only provided the necessary stamp of objective authority, but also suggested that societal conditions were unlikely to change, and indeed it was futile to even attempt to effect change, because of immutable biological factors. Who could argue with the raw scientific data? Fortunately, many people eventually did, which launched a concerted effort to refute the pseudoscience of IQ testing.

For example, noted educator Horace Mann Bond wrote about a differential between the IQ scores of northern and southern blacks and surmised that any differences were not due to the biological superiority of northern blacks. Instead, Bond concluded that the differential was likely attributable to the difference in expenditures in northern and southern schools. Similarly, psychologist, Otto Klineberg, using army tests, compared the median scores of blacks from four northern states to whites from four southern states and found that blacks had outscored whites on these mental tests.[18] The fact that these allegedly scientific claims were so easily refuted reflects the general theme of the Mensh & Mensh book that "[w]hile science advances to higher and higher stages, pseudoscience can produce no more than variations on one or another fallacious theme."[19] Pseudoscience also has the capacity to produce a great deal of seemingly intelligent verbiage to support it. For instance, Mensh & Mensh point to a statement made by Harvard psychologist, Edmund Boring, as an example of the arrogant and nonsensical lan-

---

degenerate offspring for a crime, or to let them starve for their imbecility, society can prevent those who are manifestly unfit from continuing their kind.... Three generations of imbeciles are enough.
Buck v. Bell, 274 U.S. 200, 207 (1927) (speaking about Carrie Buck, whom Justice Holmes described as the daughter of a feebleminded mother and the mother of an illegitimate feebleminded daughter).
    18. Mensh & Mensh, THE IQ MYTHOLOGY, at 32.
    19. *Id.* at 42.

guage offered in support of intelligence testing. Boring observed that "intelligence as a measurable capacity must at the start be defined as the capacity to do well on an intelligence test. Intelligence is what the test tests."[20]

Despite Boring's patently circular rationale for IQ testing, Mensh & Mensh conclude, as have others, that the core difficulty with IQ testing is that the tests are obviously lacking in objectivity and simply do not measure intelligence, to the extent that intelligence can even be defined. Instead, the tests measure "surrogates" for intelligence "namely the skills, information, and social values called for by the test questions."[21] Because the tests are often developed by white middle-class men and women, it is perhaps not surprising that the tested skills, information and social values are tied to a white middle-class norm. Realistically then, the majority of IQ tests simply measure one's relative position vis-à-vis the established cultural norm and prove absolutely nothing about one's specific capacity to learn and be successful in life. More importantly, however, because these norms are mutable and are developing and changing over time throughout the larger society, IQ tests cannot legitimately attribute differences in abilities to reflect current cultural norms to genetics or biological inferiority/superiority. To put it simply, the IQ test standards were developed by whites, incorporated white values, skills and information and then measured minority groups' deviation from this predetermined norm. The results were then said to prove the inferiority of those who deviated from the norm. As Andrew J. Strenio pointed out in his book, *The Testing Trap*, "[we] consciously and deliberately select questions so that the kind of people who scored low on the pretest will score low in subsequent tests. We are imposing our will on the outcome."[22]

Although the various scientific bases for IQ differentials between the races have been consistently and often successfully challenged, IQ test results have nevertheless become a focal point in the ongoing battle to obtain equal educational opportunity for black students.

---

20. *Id.* at 47.
21. *Id.* at 48.
22. Andrew J. Strenio, Jr., The Testing Trap 95 (1981).

This means that in the classroom setting black students potentially face two equally negative outcomes because of IQ testing pseudoscience. In one scenario, educational goals and expectations for black students are essentially abandoned because of a belief that biological inferiority is immutable. In most cases, however, black students are simply "tracked" to less academically rigorous programs, which places them at a tremendous long-term disadvantage with respect to education, employment and overall earning capacity.[23] Much of the academic tracking of black students came to the forefront after the official order to desegregate public schools in the United States Supreme Court opinion in *Brown v. Board of Education*. Rather than comply with the Court's order, many schools began a system of IQ testing that naturally purported to objectively place students on various tracks according to their known abilities. Hence, the pseudoscience of IQ testing was not only used to circumvent an order issued by the highest court in the land, but was again used to blatantly perpetuate the racial bias that had already doomed black students to a poor education and even poorer outlooks for the future.

Typical of the tracking phenomena was the case of Larry P. v. Riles, which challenged the use of standardized intelligence tests that tracked black children into special classes for the educable mentally retarded (EMR).[24] The EMR classes in the California school system specifically targeted children considered incapable of academic learning in regular classes and were designed to teach them minimal social adjustment and economic usefulness (shades of Binet). A subsequent review of the program determined that, from 1968–1977, black children were significantly overrepresented in EMR classes, which led the plaintiffs in the Riles case to argue that this could not be the result of chance. In response to this claim, the defendants theorized that because there is a higher incidence of mental retardation among the black population, this disproportion would "naturally" result in an overenrollment of black students in the EMR classes.

---

23. Additionally, tracking often stigmatizes students to such a degree that even those who have the potential to achieve begin to believe otherwise, thus resulting in a self-fulfilling prophecy.

24. Larry P. v. Riles, 793 F.2d 969 (9th Cir. 1984).

Upon hearing the case, the district court found that IQ tests were either determinative or pervasive in the placement of black children in special EMR classes. Addressing the validity of using IQ tests as a sole criterion in the EMR placement process, the court concluded that:

> the tests were never designed to eliminate cultural biases against black children; it was assumed that black children were less intelligent than whites.... The tests were standardized and developed on an all-white population and naturally their scientific validity is questionable for culturally different groups.[25]

The court also observed that although IQ tests were subsequently standardized to eliminate *gender* bias, "[n]o such modification on racial grounds has ever been tried before by the testing companies... the experts have from the beginning been willing to tolerate or even encourage tests that portray minorities, especially blacks, as intellectually inferior."[26] The court also rejected the defendants' argument that the parents of the EMR students had consented to their children's enrollment in the classes, thereby overcoming any deficiencies resulting from bias in the placement process. The court stated that "consent is rarely withheld, particularly by minorities, since the mystique of teacher authority and IQ scores tends to overwhelm parents."[27]

---

25. Larry P. v. Riles, 495 F.Supp 926, 956–57 (N.D. Cal. 1979).

26. Riles, at 955.

27. Riles, at 950 n. 51. Defendants also analogized the accepted use of testing in the employment context as a basis for arguing that predictive testing should be acceptable in the educational environment. The court rejected this argument, explaining that:

> [I]f tests can predict that a person is going to be a poor employee, the employer can legitimately deny that person a job, but if tests suggest that a young child is probably going to be a poor student, the school cannot on that basis alone deny that child the opportunity to improve and develop the academic skills necessary to success in our society. Assigning a student to an EMR class denies that child the opportunity to develop the necessary academic skills... and [is] essentially a dead-end academic track. Larry P. v. Riles, 793 F.2d 969, 980.

This is but one example of the significant negative impact the pseudoscience of IQ testing has visited upon generations of minority youth. One can only imagine the countless numbers of black citizens who have been categorized as intellectually inferior by these biased testing procedures and thereafter precluded from realizing a host of benefits, opportunities, hopes and dreams. Raymond Franklin concludes in his book *Shadows of Race and Class*:

> When one examines the long history of the misuse of biological scientism against African Americans, when one considers the history of scientists actually doctoring and falsifying their collected data to prove black inferiority, when one considers the gaps in knowledge about genetics that characterizes its use by social scientists, when one includes the large variety of ways that assumed endowment observations can be misspecified because of the prevalence of numerous environmental subtleties that are omitted from consideration, one reaches a simple conclusion: racially biased scientists are normal. Like ordinary folk living in a racially charged and stratified society, they have their racialist theories that relate to social policies and practices. Unlike ordinary citizens who are upfront about their racial sentiments, hereditarians are sinister; they use the scientific enterprise as a screen to conceal biases. Since racially biased scientists are active respondents contributing to a racially biased social and class structure, changing the former must go hand in hand with changing the latter.[28]

The Tuskegee "Experiment"

One of the saddest chapters in the history of what Franklin describes as our racially charged and stratified society involves what has become known as the Tuskegee Syphilis Experiment. This pseu-

---

28. Franklin, SHADOWS, at 68.

doscientific investigation of the long term effects of syphilis allowed doctors and scientists to implement their racialist theories while jeopardizing the lives of 600 black men in Alabama. What began as a syphilis "control" program eventually devolved into a deadly syphilis "experiment" in which poor, uneducated black men were given meager sums in exchange for participating in a study that essentially left their syphilitic conditions untreated for purposes of "research." This notorious study began during a period of what has been referred to as racialized medicine. As James H. Jones describes in his book, *Bad Blood: The Tuskegee Syphilis Experiment*, in the nineteenth century, physicians, as a group, were subject to the dominant culture thinking about race and "did a great deal to bolster and elaborate racist attitudes."[29] Just as in the case of IQ testing, physicians of the time had a vested interest in maintaining the existing social order and "medical discourses on the peculiarities of blacks offered, among other things, a pseudoscientific rationale for keeping blacks in their places."[30] Additionally, it was not uncommon for physicians to define black health problems in racial terms. Indeed, "[s]ome physicians of the day were overtly judgmental and spoke of blacks as having earned their illnesses as just recompense for wicked lifestyles" and concluded that blacks had become a "notoriously syphilis soaked race."[31]

The public health movement toward the end of the nineteenth century gave hope that not only would society's general health standards improve, but that blacks would also benefit from the renewed emphasis on medicine. Nowhere was this hope more evident than Macon County, Alabama, where, in 1930, blacks accounted for 82% of the 27,000 residents. Because extreme poverty left most of the residents without sufficient resources to obtain regular medical treatment, diseases such as syphilis were rampant among the black community. Thus, when the United States government stepped in with a syphilis "control" program in Macon County, public officials welcomed them with open arms and black residents willingly cooperated with the program. This was not the traditional physician/pa-

29. JAMES H. JONES, BAD BLOOD: THE TUSKEGEE SYPHILIS EXPERIMENT 17 (1993).
30. *Id.*
31. *Id.* at 22.

tient relationship however because rather than "burden" their syphilitic black patients with detailed explanations of their illnesses and treatment plans, government officials simply told them they were testing for "bad blood," a confusing euphemism that masked the true focus of the control program. Concerning this failure to disclose the serious nature of the black patients' illnesses, Jones notes:

> How was syphilis to be controlled among people who were not informed that they suffered from a specific, definable disease; who were not informed the disease was contagious; who were not told that the disease was transmitted through sexual intercourse; and who were not informed that in congenital syphilis the germ passes from the mother through the placenta to the fetus?[32]

The answer is that such explanations were simply not necessary given the very limited focus of the original program. Officials merely wanted to demonstrate to state and local officials that the disease *could be* discovered and controlled rather than educating black patients about the nature and extent of this potentially deadly disease. In other words, health officials were primarily interested in determining the prevalence of the disease and only secondarily concerned with treatment.[33] Arguably, this dispassionate attitude of doctors toward the obviously ill and poorly educated black patients set the stage for the next step in the syphilis control program: The Tuskegee Syphilis Experiment.

At the conclusion of the control program, public health officials discovered to their surprise that the rate of syphilis in Macon County was an alarming thirty-six percent.[34] Nevertheless, due to a

---

32. *Id.* at 73–4.

33. In fact, it was estimated that approximately 1400 black patients were *admitted* to treatment during the control program. Although about 33 of them received some minor treatment, not one of the patients ever received the full course of treatment for syphilis despite being diagnosed with the disease. *Id.* at 92.

34. An ironic twist to the prevalence of syphilis in black residents in Macon County was that the county sat in the shadow of the prestigious Tuskegee Institute, which was founded by Booker T. Washington and later became one of the leading black educational institutions of the time.

severe lack of state financial and personnel resources to support a larger syphilis health care program in Alabama, the initial syphilis control program was terminated. It was, however, deemed a partial success because the control program demonstrated that blacks could be treated for syphilis on a community wide basis. Indeed, this control program was the precursor for the nationwide syphilis health program that began in the late 1930s.

In the midst of this burgeoning emphasis on syphilis treatment and control, public health officials made the calculated decision to return to Tuskegee and Macon County, but this time for quite a different reason. Because they already knew Macon County had a high percentage of *untreated* syphilitic blacks, public officials believed that Macon County offered "an unparalleled opportunity for the study of the effect of untreated syphilis."[35] Apparently, actually treating the affected population was not an option because of severely limited resources, but studying the population could at least offer some return on the investment of time and effort expended during the earlier control program.

But why was such a risky study even necessary? Dr. Taliaferro Clark, who initiated the idea for the Tuskegee Syphilis Study, believed a great deal could be learned about the course of syphilis by observing untreated blacks. To be fair, there had been at least two previous studies of untreated syphilis, one of which, the Oslo Study, focused upon white subjects. However, one major difference between these studies and the Tuskegee study was that the prior studies were retrospective in the sense that the researchers used case studies as a basis for their analysis rather than actual ongoing examinations with human patients. Yet, despite the obvious risks presented, Dr. Clark was encouraged by the opportunity to take a "new approach" to the study of untreated syphilis and argued that "it was time for a further study of the effect of untreated syphilis in the human economy among people now living and engaged in daily pursuits."[36] Moreover, Clark knew that the key to a successful experiment of this deadly nature was gaining the confidence of local government offi-

---

35. Jones, BAD BLOOD, at 91.
36. *Id.* at 94.

cials and residents. With that in mind, he set about devising a plan to present the experiment as a *continuation* of the syphilis control program and enlist the aid of the Tuskegee Institute as a means of making the "experiment" more palatable to the local community. He succeeded at both.[37]

In terms of scientific methods and processes, the stated goal of the Tuskegee study was to demonstrate that syphilis affected blacks and whites differently, although there was no legitimate scientific basis for such a belief and treatment for the disease in both groups was the same. Nevertheless, the study protocol was based upon this pseudoscientific notion and Dr. Clark was given virtually unfettered discretion as he set out to explore untreated or partially treated syphilis in blacks in Macon county. What is particularly noteworthy about this poorly designed racist study is that, despite obvious flaws in the scientific basis and design of the experiment, no one ever questioned the ethics or morality of the proposed study and Dr. Clark's "experiment" was approved and implemented with the full cooperation of the federal government and local officials in Macon County, Alabama.

As history now reveals, what began as a 6–8 month study lasted forty years. During that time, there were numerous personnel changes, the validity and value of the study were repeatedly criticized, subjects participating in the study dropped out of sight or died, subjects were lied to about the extent and purposes of the study, and yet the Tuskegee syphilis experiment continued. As Jones observes, it made little difference who was at the helm [of the Public Health Service], the study persisted "through the national syphilis campaign, WWII, the development of penicillin and public reaction to the Nuremberg trials."[38] The Tuskegee study had become a sacred cow within the Public Health Service and each successive wave of

---

37. In retrospect, the latter success is undoubtedly a particularly painful episode in the history of the Tuskegee Institute because the institution founded by Booker T. Washington as a place to assist in the advancement of black people was a conscious aider and abettor in the abuse and mistreatment of hundreds of ailing blacks in Macon County.

38. Jones, BAD BLOOD, at 180.

doctors and civil servants who came in contact with the study simply did their jobs without any apparent sense of moral or ethical concern. Jones does however describe one instance in which a government official was "skeptical and troubled about the scientific merits of the study and somewhat uneasy about its moral implications as well."[39] These concerns focused on the fact that the study was procedurally and conceptually weak because, among other things, some of the men in the study had actually been treated for syphilis while in the study. These concerns were easily assuaged though and, in the end, the government official merely recommended that the study be "scientifically improved."

The amorphous boundaries of the study protocol also became apparent over time as the purposes of the study mutated with the changes in personnel at the Public Health Service. At one point, a doctor associated with the study imagined even greater possibilities for the research findings and noted that "this Tuskegee project is only half realized. Its possibilities are only developing. Its conclusions will probably shed as much light on our understanding of the factors in aging and heart disease as in the problems with syphilis."[40] But perhaps one of the most egregious circumstances of willful neglect during the Tuskegee experiment came about in 1943, when it was discovered that penicillin provided effective treatment for syphilis. Those in charge of the Tuskegee experiment at that time were well aware of this new "wonder drug" for syphilis treatment. But instead of terminating the study and offering the men effective treatment, officials argued incredibly that the study had now become even more valuable because the new treatments being widely used to combat syphilis meant that never again would they have such a huge population of untreated syphilis patients to use in their experiment. So the men in the study went untreated even though effective treatment was widely available.

At this point, one might be tempted to question whether these men were *involuntarily* being used as subjects in this study. After all, weren't they aware of their illnesses? Couldn't they have learned of the use of

---

39. *Id.* at 181.
40. *Id.* at 184.

penicillin as a treatment for syphilis and chosen to receive such treatment? Shouldn't they shoulder some of the blame for the long-term nature of this study? These questions touch upon the complex issue of *informed* consent to participation in medical experiments. Almost certainly, poverty and ignorance played a major role in the men's participation in the study. The financial incentives were minimal, yet given the stark nature of their daily existence, an occasional hot lunch, periodic physical examinations and a burial stipend may have seemed like plenitude. Moreover, it is now widely believed that these particular black men were chosen because they were "poor, illiterate and completely at the mercy of the 'benevolent' Public Health Service."[41] Under these circumstances, the subjects could hardly be expected to protest the treatment or seek other options when many didn't completely understand the nature of their illnesses and may have believed that they were actually being treated while in the study.

The issue of race was also a driving factor in selecting "patients" for this deadly experiment. When the experiment began, it had been more than sixty years since the Emancipation Proclamation officially freed the slaves, but the United States was still in the midst of a legalized system of segregation known as Jim Crow. This "official" form of segregation continued the dehumanization of blacks even though the yokes of slavery had been released. Thus, it can scarcely be denied that racism played a significant role in selecting and keeping 600 black men in a woefully unscientific and deadly study for forty years. In fact, when the study was finally revealed, many observed that this type of thing could only happen to blacks because America's racist society completely disregarded the humanity of its black citizens. As a result, most white Americans could not have cared less that scientists were engaged in a scientifically, morally and ethically unsound experiment that unnecessarily exposed hundreds of black men to a potentially deadly disease.

The Tuskegee study demonstrated that, once again, science could be manipulated in the shameful pursuit of the oppression of blacks in America. Moreover, in the Tuskegee case, the "scientific" study continued for an unusually lengthy period with the express or tacit ap-

---

41. *Id.* at 14.

proval of several large institutions including a United States government agency *despite its dubious validity*. Given these circumstances, it is hardly surprising that black people regard scientific and technological advance with a marked degree of suspicion and, in some cases, outright fear. When your intellectual capacities are consistently challenged and denigrated with "science" and when your physical being is regarded as less than human and exposed to the untreated rigors of a deadly disease in the name of "science," fear of science and technology is not unwarranted paranoia, but a matter of sheer survival.

Against this backdrop, an aura of mistrust has developed in the black community where matters of science and technology are concerned. As Jones describes in the final chapter of his book, one of the ramifications of the Tuskegee study is that many blacks mistrust and/or fear doctors. Additionally, newly discovered diseases are regarded with the utmost suspicion, particularly if the diseases tend to impact races or certain populations differently. For example, the advent of AIDS engendered widespread speculation among blacks that the disease was created by the government in order to intentionally infect black people. In other words, AIDS was considered a form of government supported conspiratorial genocide. While many may scoff at this seemingly ridiculous notion, one need only consider the history of race relations, government sanctioned discrimination, and the manipulation of science to suit racist agendas to understand the foundations that underlie these beliefs. This long history of racism also leaves many blacks particularly susceptible to belief in myths and "urban legends," especially those that purport to describe instances of discrimination or oppression.

As Patricia Turner discusses in her book, *I Heard It Through The Grapevine*, "[r]umors and contemporary legends capture modern anxieties by commenting on the effects of urbanization, mass society, technology and strained ethnic relations."[42] This type of storytelling is an attempt "by people to negotiate their current reality, and to deal with the changes in their personal environment."[43] For

---

42. Patricia A. Turner, I Heard It Through the Grapevine 126 (1993).

43. *Id.* at 82.

blacks, of course, this current reality invariably involves racism, which increasingly occurs covertly and frequently leaves an informational void in terms of explaining biased outcomes. This vacuum is usually filled with suspicion and rumor that, not surprisingly, often confirms the subject's own view of the world.

For example, Turner describes a rumor that spread throughout the black community alerting those in the community that a particular fried chicken fast food restaurant was owned by the Ku Klux Klan. According to the rumor, the Klan was adding an ingredient to the chicken recipe to "make black men sterile and effectively wipe out the continuation of the black community."[44] This persistent rumor illustrates several themes. First, there is a pervasive belief by many blacks that their physical beings are regarded as less than human and therefore subject to physical, mental or chemical attack at any time by the powers that be. Second, as Turner points out, this type of rumor allows the potential victims of racism to name their aggressor, in this case, the KKK.[45] As noted above, since modern day racism is primarily covert, the sources of racist attack can be easily disguised. This type of rumor, which names a historical enemy of black people as the aggressor, gives those spreading the rumor the sense of empowerment that comes from being able to specifically identify their attacker. Finally, by sharing this with fellow black people, a feeling of community is created through the shared struggle for survival in a racist society.[46]

Turner also describes some common threads that appear to determine when a particular product will be targeted for rumor (and informal boycott) in the black community. According to Turner, the product price, its potential risks and a perceived negligible utility often coalesce to form a web of suspicion around a product and contribute to the black public's wariness of that product.[47] In other words, when the costs and risks associated with a product outweigh its perceived usefulness to black consumers, the product will likely

---

44. *Id.* at 105.
45. *Id.* at 106.
46. *Id.* at 106–7.
47. *Id.* at 174–9.

be avoided. To illustrate this avoidance phenomena, Turner cites the example of Reebok International, an athletic shoe retailer that was beleaguered in the late 1980s by rumors that the company was owned by South Africans who were surreptitiously seeking to profit from the sale of shoes that were very popular in the United States, particularly in the black community. In fact, the shoes were so popular that some in the black community were afraid to wear them outdoors for fear that their lives would be at risk if someone else wanted the coveted shoes badly enough.

Turner theorizes that the Reebok rumor evolved because the escalating price of the shoes at the time, coupled with the risk of wearing them (potential death), exceeded their desirability and usefulness to many black consumers, thus creating a situation where rumors about the product were likely to develop. As Turner points out, "one way for folk to show their concern about a desirable commodity with dubious practical value, particularly in a community whose financial resources are limited, is to subscribe to and circulate rumors that diminish the product's attraction."[48] It is clear then that "the folk imagination does not randomly identify products to avoid. A logical and practical process is at work, with the power of folk belief behind it."[49] Indeed. The next section will adopt Turner's price, risk, utility equation to demonstrate how a similar logical and practical process imbued with the power of folk belief may very well explain the black community's avoidance of technology.

Overcoming the Avoidance Factor

Turner's theory on the process of how rumors develop when set forth as a formula is as follows:

Price + Risk > Utility = Rumor[50]

---

48. *Id.* at 98.
49. *Id.* at 179.
50. *Id.* at 174.

Rumor, of course, then leads to avoidance or, at minimum, a diminished appreciation for the product. Let's examine each of the elements of this formula as it might be applied in the area of computers and technology.

Price

Several years ago, a reliable desktop computer system may have required expenditures ranging from $2–3000. Today, such systems can be purchased for approximately $900 brand new with all the modern bells and whistles. In order to realize the full potential of computer ownership in the digital age and take advantage of the Internet and e-commerce, most users would need to add the cost of an Internet Service Provider (ISP) to the total cost of owning a computer system. Today, ISP accounts range in price from free to approximately $21.95 for unlimited monthly usage.[51] With a typical ISP account, users gain access to the World Wide Web (WWW) and other Internet communication tools, obtain one or more e-mail accounts, and are allotted space on the ISP's server to establish a personal webpage. At first glance, these prices certainly seem reasonable and well within reach of consumers with even modest incomes. It appears then that the low cost of owning a computer and accessing the Internet should be a positive factor in the price/risk/utility formula. However, upon closer examination, this may not necessarily be the case.

Although economic factors contributing to the technology gap will be explored in more detail in Chapter 2, a brief discussion at this point will be helpful in analyzing why even the low cost of computer ownership may not translate into increased ownership in the black community. As Melvin L. Oliver and Thomas M. Shapiro note in their book *Black Wealth/White Wealth: A New Perspective On Racial Inequality*, despite the progress that blacks have made over the past 40 years, "poor education, high joblessness, low incomes, and the subsequent hardships of poverty, family and community

---

51. The free ISPs are good deals for those who don't mind viewing an onslaught of advertisements as they surf the Internet.

instability, and welfare dependency plague many African Americans."[52] As a further commentary on the dire economic circumstances of blacks in America, Oliver & Shapiro point out that nearly one out of three blacks lives in poverty and one in four remains outside private health insurance or Medicaid coverage.[53] Given this economic reality, it is hardly surprising that there exists a sharp disparity between the incomes and wealth of blacks and whites. To illustrate this disproportion, Oliver & Shapiro discuss the results of the 1988 Survey of Income and Program Participation (SIPP), which showed that for every dollar earned by white households, black households earn sixty-two cents. Additionally, whites possess nearly twelve times as much median net worth as blacks, or $43,800 versus $3,700. Finally, the SIPP revealed that the average white household controls $6,999 in *net* financial assets while the average black household possesses no *net* financial assets at all.[54]

To say that the average black household maintains no net financial assets paints a very precarious and disturbing picture of the day to day, month to month existence of these black families. Indeed, the SIPP data showed that this resource deprivation is so severe among black families that only eleven percent of black children grow up in households with enough net financial assets to survive three months of no income at poverty level. This means very simply that the overwhelming majority of black households are entirely dependent upon an income stream that is consumed each month and does not allow for any significant savings or diverse asset accumulation. In these types of "touch and go" financial circumstances, when emergencies arise, the family is typically required to borrow from relatives or "rob Peter to pay Paul" in order to meet their financial obligations. Consequently, it is highly unlikely that purchases will be made when the risk of owning the product is perceived to be high and the utility is believed to be low, *no matter how reasonable the cost of the item*. Each additional purchase must be justified according to the price/risk/utility formula or it simply will not become part of the family's asset

---

52. MELVIN L. OLIVER & THOMAS M. SHAPIRO, BLACK WEALTH/WHITE WEALTH: A NEW PERSPECTIVE ON RACIAL INEQUALITY 24 (1995).
53. *Id.* at 24.
54. *Id.* at 86.

base. Thus, the price of an item is inextricably intertwined with the perceived risk of owning it and its potential usefulness. But, what risk could possibly arise from owning a personal computer or accessing the Internet? After all, advertisements continually prevail upon people to purchase home computers and join the digital revolution. As discussed in the next section, the *perceived* risks to black people in owning personal computers are partially rooted in reality and partially a painful byproduct of unpleasant historical experiences with science and technology.

The Risk to Privacy

It was recently discovered that the FBI is using a software system designed to allow law enforcement personnel to intercept and analyze vast amounts of e-mail being transmitted over the Internet. The system, known as "Carnivore," is placed with an ISP (usually the ISP being utilized by the suspected criminal), which then allows it to scan all incoming and outgoing e-mail intended for the target of a criminal probe. While Carnivore is in place on the ISP network, it is completely controlled by the law enforcement agency that requested its placement. According to opponents of the system, although law enforcement should limit its interception to the incoming and outgoing e-mail of the suspect, while in place, Carnivore is capable of intercepting all of the e-mail traffic on its host ISP. Thus, users of the ISP must simply trust that the government will limit its activities to the target of the criminal probe.

In another recent news item, it was reported that Microsoft intentionally left open a "back door" in its software to enable the National Security Agency (NSA) to access the software at will. This back door would, in effect, allow anyone with access to an individual's personal computer to decrypt anything on that computer and also modify the operating system. Although Microsoft has vehemently denied that the NSA would ever have a key to the "back door" of the software, the key was mysteriously named NSAKEY.

Finally, in another privacy invasion incident, the White House recently revealed that it might have violated federal privacy guidelines by allowing its office of National Drug Control Policy to use software that tracked computer users who viewed the government's anti-drug messages on the Internet. Apparently, if web surfers visited the National Drug Control website, a "cookie" was placed on their computer systems that tracked their subsequent Internet travels. Although the purported reason for the tracking effort was to measure which ads were more effective in sending users to anti-drug sites, the use of cookies to track sites visited by Internet users gives rise to serious concerns that the government may indeed be compiling this information for other less savory purposes.

With the infinite uses and misuses of Internet technology occurring today, there are without a doubt a plethora of existing and anticipated technological instruments designed specifically to intrude upon the privacy of online users. Cynics among us might respond: "So what? Using the Internet is not a private endeavor anyway. By the very nature of the construction of the Internet, it is apparent that online activities are potentially open to view by others. It's the chance we take to have access to this technology. Besides, those who aren't doing anything wrong will have nothing to hide."

Addressing the latter issue first, there are millions of people engaged in legitimate activities who would rather not have their activities tracked. Quite simply, they believe that where they go on the Internet and who they correspond with by e-mail is not anyone else's business. Second, while using the Internet implies a certain willingness to consent to a lesser expectation of privacy, most users probably expect that whatever private information is revealed about them is eventually disseminated throughout the ether to become part of the vast anonymous jungle of bits and bytes. Few expect that personal information will be compiled and uniquely tied to them to create a "profile" of online behavior for marketing purposes or otherwise. The United States Supreme Court has addressed this privacy issue in the case of *United States Department of Justice v. Reporters Committee for Freedom of the Press*.[55] Although this case did not deal specifically with computer technology, the Court discussed general privacy interests that may be implicated when the government or

---

55. United States Department of Justice v. Reporters Committee for Freedom of the Press, 489 U.S. 749 (1989).

other entities compile databases of personal information. The Court began by recognizing that "both the common law and the literal understanding of privacy encompass the individual's control of information concerning his or her person."[56] Next, in determining what constitutes private information, the Court noted that Webster's dictionary defined as private any information "intended for or restricted to the use of a particular person or group or class of persons; not freely available to the public."[57] The Court then summarized this broad concept of personal privacy by observing that simply because "an event is not wholly private does not mean that an individual has no interest in limiting its disclosure or dissemination of the information."[58]

Applying this concept to online activities suggests that one could reasonably conclude that Internet users implicitly "agree" that some information about them will be revealed while online, but they maintain a privacy interest in that information to the extent that they do not agree that the information will be further compiled and disseminated without their knowledge and consent. In other words, there is some degree of privacy afforded by the bits and pieces of information that are released online incrementally and potentially forgotten over time. But, if an entity is collecting these bits and pieces of information and compiling them to create online profiles uniquely tied to individual users, then the potential loss of privacy posed by this aggregate information is much greater than any loss associated with the intermittent release of the bits and pieces.

When these actual and potential privacy breaches are viewed by black Americans through a historical prism of mistrust in the areas of science and technology, the risk of owning a personal computer and accessing the Internet is magnified. Indeed, the risk may be perceived as the equivalent of forfeiting one's right to personal privacy, particularly when the inner workings of computers are largely incomprehensible to the average layperson. This is certainly not meant to imply that black Americans have more to hide

---

56. *Id.* at 763.
57. *Id.*
58. *Id.* at 770.

and are therefore more concerned about privacy than the average computer user. Instead, it is to suggest that because of a unique historical perspective, blacks are more likely to have a heightened sense of awareness where personal privacy issues are concerned and, accordingly, act more vigilantly when it comes to protecting against unwarranted governmental intrusion into their private lives. To the extent that computer technology is associated with the intolerable risk of invading personal privacy, blacks are less likely to purchase and utilize such devices no matter what the price. Moreover, because the risk is so high, the combination of price and risk is likely to outweigh utility (discussed below) in the minds of many blacks, thereby leading to avoidance of the technology and the development of rumors. For example, it is not uncommon to hear that some black Americans refuse to own computers because they believe that the government or some other intrusive agency will be able to watch them and monitor their physical movements through their computer screens.

Thus, in order to increase black ownership of personal computers and increase black participation in the online arena, it is not enough to simply reduce the price of personal computers. Additional steps must be taken to reduce the actual and perceived risks to personal privacy. This will require the enactment and enforcement of laws designed to protect everyone's privacy in the digital age, as well as stiff sanctions for those who violate those laws. It will also require education and training to empower online users in ways that enable them to protect their personal information without sacrificing their enjoyment of technology resources.

Utility: But What Good Is A Computer?

This question is likely posed by many of the technology uninitiated everyday. Many people simply cannot envision how a computer can fit comfortably into their lives, especially when their daily routine involves a complex juggling of family, work, school, church and other social obligations. How can a stationary plastic box with an assortment of tangled wires make any of this more efficient and convenient? Although the utility of computers and other digital technology will be discussed in detail in Chapters 4, 5, and 6, at this point, it will simply be noted that the issue of utility is largely an educational process. To many, computers are a mystery; a mystery that many blacks are afraid to unravel because of the aforementioned risks. Uncloaking this mystery means explaining the nature of computers and what they can accomplish in layperson's language *and* making it relevant to daily experience.

For example, the cell phone revolution appears to have crossed all racial and class boundaries in its infiltration of modern society. Based upon general observation, it seems that, on average, blacks are probably just as likely to own or have access to cell phones as whites. What accounts for the fact that the black population seems to have embraced this technology with very little trepidation? The answer may be found once again in the price/risk/utility formula. While the price of obtaining a cell phone and service varies, there is enough competition in the wireless market to enable practically anyone to find a wireless phone and calling plan to fit their budget. This ease of ownership makes price an attractive factor in the equation. There are certain risks associated with cell phone usage such as driver distraction and a purported link to increased risks for certain cancers. These risks probably seem too remote, however, and either do not evoke a response based upon historical baggage or any such response is overcome by the usefulness and relevance of the product in daily life. The ability to communicate with friends and relatives while "on the go" is a valuable commodity to all sectors of society because it makes navigating the logistical complexities of life a bit more manageable. Having the ability to communicate at will is efficient, convenient and enhances feelings of connectedness with one's family and friends. All of this translates into greater acceptance of this technology by members of the black community. Moreover, in its initial stages, cell phone technology was likely an easier "sell" in terms of persuading people of all races to adopt the technology because it is simply a more convenient offshoot of a device that is now fairly commonplace: the home telephone. Computers and the Internet have no such predecessor to recommend them and help facilitate overall public acceptance of the technology. Widespread acceptance of computer technology by the public, and particularly the black public, will therefore require innovative approaches that recognize the varieties of ways that people carry out their daily activities and a concerted effort to make computers and Internet technology relevant to and compatible with these activities. As mentioned earlier, Chapters 4, 5 and 6 will explore the numerous ways in which technology is enhancing lives everyday and will hopefully serve as an important step toward increasing the perception of computers as useful components in this digital age.

Chapter 2

The Economic Gap

When many people discover that there is such a term as the "digital divide" and that it is used to describe the disparity between those who have access to computer technology and those who don't, they conclude that these difference may be, in large part, the result of individual choices. That is, because computers are so reasonably priced and easily acquired today, anyone who doesn't own a computer is simply making a choice not to own one. This argument is appealing because it suggests that the digital divide can be remedied by somehow getting people to make better choices concerning the allocation of their financial resources. It is also appealing because it contains some degree of truth. For example, it is true that over the past several years, the prices of personal computers have dramatically decreased and, as a result, basic computer systems are well within the financial reach of many people at various socioeconomic levels. It is also true that many people who have the financial means to purchase computers choose not to do so and instead allocate their resources toward other purchases. However, making goods available at reduced prices doesn't necessarily mean that more people will be attracted to those products. Similarly, because people choose not to purchase a product at the reduced price doesn't mean that they are actively rejecting that product, i.e., saying "I never want to own a personal computer." As discussed in Chapter 1, the decision not to purchase a personal computer may simply mean that the knowledge base to appreciate the additional benefit that product would produce is lacking.[1]

---

1. Of course, this may lead some to conclude that such uninformed people are victims of their own laziness and lack of intellectual curiosity. This response begs the question, however, because if a product is not *per-*

In some cases, however, even supplying the knowledge base will not be sufficient to alleviate the intractable economic resource issues that plague some segments of the population. Simply put, for certain people, everyday life is a chronic struggle for survival at subsistence level and severe economic deprivation does not permit them to see and plan very much beyond their own limited conditions. Bleak economic circumstances in a country that places so much emphasis on the acquisition of wealth and income also tends to create a sense of alienation, which negatively impacts self-perception and contributes to the "us vs. them" "have vs. have-not" dichotomy. When viewed through this prism of mutual exclusion, the "haves" are perceived as living comfortably and capable of acquiring a vast array of resources, including those that allow them to take part in the digital revolution. In contrast, the "have-nots" are viewed as existing in chronically unstable environments piecing together meager resources just to keep roofs over their heads and food on the table. The have-nots cannot afford to sacrifice the time or financial resources to learn or adapt to new technology, and would likely consider computer technology as just another financial burden that would not yield any immediate potential for increased financial stability. This is a particularly sad reality because just the opposite is likely to be true. While computers and the Internet are certainly no panacea for all of society's ills, these technological resources do have demonstrated potential to assist people in developing and improving their skills, knowledge, marketability and income. Ironically, those who could most benefit from these resources are often foreclosed from acquiring or accessing them. What accounts for this economic disparity that ultimately restricts the future choices and opportunities of some segments of the population? This is, of course, a complex question that permits no easy answers. But, just as in Chapter 1, a brief foray into the past may help to provide perspective.

---

ceived as valuable, then very little time and effort will be expended in attempting to explore its usefulness.

The Economics of Slavery

The ancestors of most black Americans began life in this country in bondage. As such, they were afforded dual status, first as chattel (or property) and second as persons. Kenneth Stampp, in his book, *The Peculiar Institution*, discusses the difficulties that arose from trying to treat people as property and persons. According to Stampp, "legislators and magistrates were caught in a dilemma whenever they found that the slave's status as property was incompatible with his status as a person. Individual masters struggled with this dilemma in different ways, some conceding much to the dictates of humanity, others demanding the utmost return from their investment."[2] But, "throughout the ante-bellum South, the cold language of statutes and judicial decisions made it evident that, legally, the slave was less a person than a thing."[3] In his capacity as property, Stampp observes, a slave was unable to acquire title to property in any manner or be a party to a contract. He could not be a party to a lawsuit nor give competent testimony in a court case unless it involved another slave. Additionally, "[h]e had no civil rights, no political rights, no claim to his time, [and] no freedom of movement."[4] In strict accordance with the law, slaves were also physically treated as property. They were "bartered, deeded, devised, pledged, seized and auctioned." They were also awarded as prizes in lotteries, tendered as payment for gambling debts and presented as gifts to children. As Stampp concludes, "[i]n all these ways the slave as property clearly had priority over the slave as person."[5]

To further emphasize the legalized nature of the slave's property status, each slave state enacted a comprehensive slave code. These codes permitted masters to discipline rebellious slaves and, in sharp (albeit self-serving) contrast to the general view of slaves as property, most codes considered slaves as thinking, morally responsible beings for purposes of assessing culpability for criminal conduct.

---

2. KENNETH M. STAMPP, THE PECULIAR INSTITUTION 192 (1989).
3. *Id.* at 193.
4. *Id.* at 198.
5. *Id.* at 201–204.

On the plantation, in exchange for the slave's back-breaking, sunup to sundown labor and utter submission, the slave master was required to provide very little. Most supplied just the bare necessities to keep their bondsmen minimally comfortable and capable of working. Indeed, the expenses paid for the food, clothing, shelter and medical care of slaves was considered the slave's "wage" according to Stampp. As far as opportunities to earn additional income, Stampp notes that the pittance provided by the master assured that most slaves would continually live at subsistence level. Furthermore, "[u]nlike the free laborer, the average slave could not attain an appreciably higher living standard, no matter how hard he strived. The slave's labor was controlled labor: his bargaining power was, by design, severely circumscribed. His labor was cheap labor: his compensation was, also by design, kept at a minimum."[6]

As a means of finding human dignity and self-respect in such hideously inhumane circumstances, slaves latched on to what they could. For some, this meant that they identified with and adopted the master's notion of respectability. Many carried this identification with the master's lifestyle much farther by professing an undying loyalty to their slave masters and helping to identify and discipline other slaves who did not evince such loyalty. Over time, the slave community developed its own caste structure based upon specialized tasks given them by the master. For example, artisans and domestics were considered the "aristocracy" of the slave society. As Stampp points out, this social structuring was yet another means of finding individual self-respect and represented a desire by slaves for "some recognition of their worth as individuals, if only from those in their own limited social orbit...."[7]

The forced immigration of Africans to America as slave labor also had an impact on previously established norms of behavior and social codes. In Africa, families and communities were accustomed to a "strictly regulated family life and a rigidly enforced moral code."[8] However, these standards quickly disintegrated in America, where

---

6. *Id.* at 282.
7. *Id.* at 333.
8. *Id.* at 340.

white standards of living and morality were the norm and the slave's deviance from those completely unfamiliar standards was presumptively attributed to innate and undesirable racial traits. The reality of course is that the white standards were meaningless and unintelligible to most slaves and, as a result, many existed in a cultural chaos, having been stripped of their native customs and unable to formulate a comprehensible substitute that would not simultaneously place them on the wrong end of the master's whip. To sum up this extraordinarily confusing existence, Stampp concludes that:

> The average bondsman, it would appear, lived more or less aimlessly in a bleak and narrow world. He lived in a world without schools, without books, without learned men; he knew less of the fine arts and of aesthetic values than he had known in Africa; and he found few ways to break the monotonous sameness of all his days. His world was the few square miles of earth surrounding his cabin—a familiar island beyond which were strange places.... His world was full of mysteries which he could not solve, full of forces which he could not control. And so he tended to be a fatalist and futilitarian, for nothing else could reconcile him to his life.[9]

Moving ahead to the Reconstruction Era when approximately four million slaves were accorded the title of freedmen, Melvin Oliver and Thomas Shapiro observe in their book *Black Wealth/ White Wealth: A New Perspective On Racial Inequality*, that after two and half centuries of legalized oppression, the freedmen "entered Southern society with little or no material assets."[10] At the time of emancipation, there was a widespread expectation that the newly freed slaves would be granted some remuneration in the form of property to begin their new lives. The now familiar notion of "forty acres and a mule" encapsulated the expectation that portions of the land that slaves had previously worked as bondsmen would be fairly distributed to them upon emancipation. Naturally, in the wake of

---

9. *Id.* at 361.
10. Melvin L. Oliver & Thomas M. Shapiro, Black Wealth/White Wealth: A New Perspective on Racial Inequality 13 (1995).

lingering hostilities occasioned by the Civil War, this massive redistribution of land in the South could not possibly be expected to occur voluntarily and, thus, the Southern Homestead Act of 1866 became the first major legislation to provide a legal basis for black land ownership. According to the Act, a total of forty-six million acres of public land was opened up to settlement by former slaves, "and there was every reason to believe that in reasonable time slaves would be transformed from farm laborers to yeomanry farmers."[11]

However, as has happened throughout history on so many issues related to race, the purposes and intent of the law were never satisfactorily transformed into reality. In this case, though, it seems that inadequately drafted legislation was partially responsible for this failure. For instance, instead of disqualifying former Confederate supporters from acquiring the land, the law allowed anyone who swore that they had not taken up arms against the Union to apply for a portion of the land. This oversight resulted in numerous white applicants and, in fact, one estimate places white ownership of land under the Act at 77%. Another obstacle was the continuing burden of racial prejudice and discrimination. Blacks applying for the land were often met with "illegal fees, expressly discriminatory court challenges and court decisions, and land speculators."[12]

The Freedmen's Bureau, an organization established by Congress to supervise the transition from slavery to freedom, administered many of the Reconstruction Era programs and, in the minds of many, was also to blame for their failure. According to David Lewis in *W.E.B Du Bois: Biography of a Race*, scholars of the time "condemned the Freedmen's Bureau as an unwise and maladministered experiment in racial uplift in the South. The general public blamed it for engendering harmful, unrealistic expectations of forty acres and a mule among the ex-slaves...."[13] Another considerable impediment to this massive land redistribution was the fact that President Andrew Johnson did not support the idea because he firmly believed that the newly freed slaves should pull themselves up by their

---

11. *Id.* at 14.
12. *Id.*
13. David L. Lewis, W.E.B. DuBois: Biography of a Race 283 (1993).

bootstraps. Apparently Johnson assumed that the ex-slaves could somehow miraculously achieve the American dream without the benefit of money or property and in the face of continuing racial prejudice.

Summarizing the overall impact of Reconstruction legislation and the Freedmen's Bureau on raising the economic circumstances of the newly freed slaves, one scholar noted that "[t]he tragedy of Reconstruction is the failure of the black masses to acquire land, since without the economic security provided by land ownership the freedmen were soon deprived of the political and civil rights which they had won."[14] It appears then that property ownership, the first and arguably most important avenue to economic security and racial equality, had been effectively foreclosed to the former slaves. The road to racial justice could only become infinitely more inaccessible from that point forward because although the yokes of slavery had been set aside by the Emancipation Proclamation, as W.E.B. DuBois observed, not much had really changed in the daily lives of the freed men and women. DuBois remarked:

> Slavery was not abolished even after the Thirteenth Amendment. There were four million freedmen and most of them on the same plantation, doing the same work that they did before emancipation, except as their work had been interrupted and changed by the upheaval of war. Moreover, they were getting about the same wages and apparently were going to be subject to slave codes modified only in name. There were among them thousands of fugitives in the camps of the soldiers or on the streets of the cities, homeless, sick and impoverished. They had been freed practically with no land nor money, and, save in exceptional cases, without legal status, and without protection.[15]

---

14. Claude Oubre, Forty Acres and a Mule: The Freedmen's Bureau and Black Land Ownership (1978).

15. W.E.B. DuBois, Black Reconstruction in America 188 (1962).

Exclusion from Asset Accumulation

In the face of a failed promise to redistribute land at the end of the Civil War, the majority of freed slaves went to work in the agricultural economy of the South. This provided a steady, although minimal, income for the largely uneducated black population. In *Race and Schooling in the South, 1880–1950: An Economic History*, Robert Margo describes how the odds of escaping farm work and obtaining a job in the non-farm economy was largely a function of schooling.[16] Because the quantity and quality of education was vastly different for blacks and whites in the South, blacks naturally lagged behind whites in making the transition to non-farm employment. According to Margo, "[t]he lag produced the increase in employment segregation in the South after 1900, which, in turn, was a key proximate cause of failure of the aggregate black-to-white earnings ratio to rise before World War Two."[17]

While the lack of education may be posited as one reason for the failure of black progress as the South became more industrialized, scholar Gavin Wright speculates that this outcome may also have been the result of a "larger historical process of creating a segregated society."[18] Wright theorizes that a historical pattern of employing whites in certain industries, such as the textile industry, made it unprofitable to vary from that practice, merely to employ inexperienced blacks. Instead, it was more profitable for blacks to remain in industries and "occupations," such as tobacco processing, which they had been accustomed to under slavery.[19] Of course, this practice of apportioning jobs based upon previous experience reinforced a pattern of occupational segregation, which relegated blacks to the lower paying, menial jobs and occupations. Occupational isolation in unskilled labor positions served to perpetuate the subsistence level ex-

---

16. Robert A. Margo, Race and Schooling in the South, 1880–1950 (1990).

17. *Id.* at 93.

18. Gavin Wright, Old South, New South: Revolutions in the Southern Economy Since the Civil War 197 (1986).

19. *Id.* at 189.

istence of black workers even in the midst of widespread industrialization and economic prosperity in America. After decades of stagnation in these lower echelon jobs, blacks were ill-prepared to take part in the next societal economic evolution, which Oliver & Shapiro describe as the: Suburbanization of America.[20]

Oliver & Shapiro theorize that the explosion of suburban areas and the consequent creation of the urban "ghetto" was supported by the government in three significant areas: taxation, transportation and housing. Tax policies favoring business relocation to areas outside of the central city, newly constructed freeways, and the promotion of single family detached housing enabled over thirty-five million families to leave the increasingly crowded city environment and realize the American dream of home ownership. Those taking part in this dream were, of course, *white* Americans and, as Oliver & Shapiro point out, the Federal Housing Authority (FHA) was a knowing conspirator in the systematic exclusion of blacks from this suburban expansion and access to property ownership.[21]

The FHA, charged with the responsibility of providing access to affordable housing, operated on a loan qualification premise that resulted in the utter neglect of central city communities. More specifically, when assessing mortgage loans for approval, the FHA had a "bias toward the financing of single-family detached homes over multifamily projects...a bias toward new purchases over repair of existing homes...[and used an] 'unbiased professional estimate' that made older homes and communities in which blacks...were located less likely to receive approval...."[22] While, at the time, the FHA's restrictive policies may have masqueraded as a "reasonable" response to the protection of its financial resources, these overtly biased policies had a ripple effect on the future economic advancement of the black community.[23] In a tragic repetition of the failed promises of

---

20. Oliver & Shapiro, Black Wealth/White Wealth, at 15.

21. *Id.* at 16.

22. *Id.* at 17–8.

23. Oliver & Shapiro cite one egregious example of how blacks were systematically excluded from asset accumulation opportunities. Levittown, a massive suburban development, boasted eminently affordable FHA and VHA financed housing. Yet, not a single black resident lived in Levittown. *Id.* at 18.

the Reconstruction era, black Americans were once again denied a stake in the massive distribution of property resources supported by government programs. Over time, the only assets at the disposal of blacks were what remained in the primarily urban communities in the wake of the initial waves of "white flight" to the suburbs: an aging infrastructure that offered few job opportunities and substandard housing.[24] As if to add insult to injury, lower paying jobs prevented most from acquiring even the modest housing in the central city. For some, this may have been a blessing in disguise because the rapidly deteriorating nature of the urban communities prevented those who did own property from obtaining financing to maintain their investments.

The intentional non-responsiveness of the formal financial establishments to the economic needs of black Americans gave rise to a host of "fringe banking" alternatives in the central city. Fringe banks are defined by John Caskey in his book, *Fringe Banking*, as pawn shops and commercial check-cashing outlets that "provide credit and payment services primarily to low- and moderate-income households, many of which rarely interact with the formal banking system."[25] One of the major themes in Caskey's book discusses how fringe banking is a costly alternative to the established banking system and is used primarily by families without financial savings. These households, Caskey contends, often have high debt to income ratios and/or bad credit records and, as a result, are generally excluded from mainstream consumer credit resources. To make matters worse, these households are typically headed by individuals with low incomes and low education levels who have unstable employment records.[26] Fringe banking establishments fill a banking and

---

24. Additional burdens visited upon central cities include "[s]chools, streets, transit systems, water supply sources, sewage, and terminals [that are] overworked and not properly maintained... [the disappearance of] black role models and stable social support groups... [and a tax base] forever caught between rising expenditure needs and limited sources of revenues." RAYMOND S. FRANKLIN, SHADOWS OF RACE AND CLASS 143 (1991).

25. JOHN P. CASKEY, FRINGE BANKING: CHECK-CASHING OUTLETS, PAWNSHOPS, AND THE POOR 1 (1994).

26. *Id.* at 6.

credit void for these households, albeit with steep transaction costs to a group of consumers who can least afford it. Nevertheless, because there is a pressing need for the services provided by these establishments, they experienced unprecedented growth during the 1980s.

Caskey contributes the rise in fringe banking establishments to at least two factors that are probably a direct result of the blatantly discriminatory policies of the FHA, which, in turn, resulted in stagnating and deteriorating urban communities. The first factor, the mass exodus of traditional branch banks from central city communities, left many of these areas without banking and financial services. In fact, several empirical studies confirm that areas of some large metropolitan cities with low income and/or minority populations have either fewer branch banks per capita or have experienced a disproportionate number of branch bank closings.[27] Although this factor may not completely explain the increased reliance upon fringe banking services in low-income urban areas, it does not require a leap in logic to conclude that those with limited access to traditional financial institutions are less likely to establish account relationships with those institutions.

The second contributory factor is the overall decline in incomes for those in lower paying occupations. After a period of marked improvement during the post-WWII era, the economy took a downward turn in the late 1970s. This decline resulted in a deterioration of living standards for a large number of people and many sank below the officially established poverty line for the first time in their lives. Blacks were particularly hard hit by this economic downturn. Because many working blacks were concentrated in manufacturing jobs in the steel, rubber and automobile industries, plant closings and the move toward deindustrialization left many without steady incomes.[28] Moreover, the relocation of jobs outside the central city, the shift from a goods to service industry and the need for more complex job skills created a vacuum between the skills and capabilities of many working class blacks and the realities

---

27. *Id.* at 90–7.
28. Oliver & Shapiro, BLACK WEALTH/WHITE WEALTH, at 26.

of the changing job market. The resulting lower incomes left few resources available for savings and jeopardized the creditworthiness of those who had managed to establish a modicum of financial stability. This impact not only widened the gap between the haves and have nots, but had obvious significance in terms of expanding the racial economic gap since blacks tended to fall disproportionately within the have not group. Of course, the aggregation of blacks in the have not category is no mere coincidence. Historical disadvantage almost certainly played a role in this categorization, and to the extent that society and the employment market have evolved economically over time, the systematic exclusion of blacks from the opportunities afforded by those structural changes only serves to reinforce these historical differences.[29] Indeed, as Oliver & Shapiro explain, this discriminatory process has resulted in a "racialized state," which is supported by seemingly benign social policies and legislative enactments.

For example, the Internal Revenue Code (commonly known as the federal tax code) provides a measure of "fiscal welfare" in the form of tax benefits to industries and activities that the government wishes to encourage, e.g., lower tax rates on capital gains encourages investment and deductions for home mortgages encourages home ownership. However, because many of the tax advantages in the code are asset-based, they serve to protect and benefit those who have the wherewithal to accumulate assets and wealth, and provide almost no tax relief to those with few or no assets. This results in the asset rich getting richer because tax code provisions are specifically designed to protect their income and assets, while the asset poor get poorer because they have very few options available to shield what little income they have from the full brunt of the tax code.

---

29. For example, wealth creation opportunities for blacks and whites are "structured by the intersection of class and race." While economists and other observers of the human social condition are quick to point out the disproportionate lack of desirable human capital in the black community, they usually fail to explain that these "deficiencies can be traced, in part, to barriers that denied blacks access to quality education, job training opportunities, jobs and other work-related factors." *Id.* at 37.

In the employment context, institutional racism results in the continued denial of equal opportunity for blacks. Employment discrimination, which is rarely overt today, either prevents blacks from obtaining access to meaningful employment or often mars the experience of those already in the workforce. The enforcement of antidiscrimination laws has helped in some respects, but cannot always protect against the insidious nature of covert discrimination. For example, many corporate organizations focus on "team building" and employees are encouraged to be "team players." These artificially constructed workplace bonds are thought to encourage congeniality and cooperation among employees, which will hopefully result in greater manageability and productivity for the company. When a potential employee is considered for a position, he is usually measured by how well he will "fit" with the team. Thus, it is not uncommon in some employment settings to hear those in charge of hiring reject an interviewee because he is not a "good fit" with the "team." This type of vague subjective evaluation can be highly detrimental to minorities, who are more likely to be perceived as unsuitable even though they may be qualified for the position. Seeking to maintain the "team" identity becomes a surrogate for perpetuating sameness and excluding difference whether it be racial, gender or ideological difference.

Even the dream of owning one's own business and being self-employed rings hollow for many blacks. A good idea can become a profitable idea in the hands of individuals with business savvy and access to capital. Black entrepreneurs, while not short on creativity, often lack the business know-how (which is a function of education) and the access to capital markets that are required to finance start-up businesses. Those who do manage to overcome these barriers are confronted with the reality of limited markets for their goods and a correspondingly bleak outlook for future profitability and expansion. This outcome is undoubtedly yet another vestige of slavery when blacks were not permitted to own property, much less establish their own businesses. Tragically, upon emancipation, the social construct of slavery, which ranked blacks and their efforts as inferior, remained. Therefore, those who were able to become business men and women still felt the sting of a social system that devalued them and their efforts and simply refused to support their entrepreneurial endeavors. This usually meant that black entrepreneurs' clientele was almost exclusively black and even then, black businesses were forced to compete with larger, more sophisticated white operations for the limited pool of black patrons.

Who's Got the Wealth?

Oliver & Shapiro conducted a detailed examination of the racial disparities in wealth acquisition in America. To begin, they defined wealth as "a stock of assets owned at a particular time...a special form of money that is not used to buy milk and shoes and other life necessities. More often it is used to create opportunities, secure a desired stature or standard of living...."[30] The study of wealth accumulation is important because it can provide insights into economic stability. More importantly, it can reveal a great deal about how families allocate their resources, which yields critical insights into what kinds of assets are available to the family at a given time and how they prioritize present and future expenditures. Using wealth as an indicator of economic stability reveals that even blacks who might be categorized as "middle class" are nevertheless very asset poor and owe their middle class designation to *income* rather than *assets*. This places them in a somewhat precarious financial position because they must rely upon income and consequently job security to meet immediate and future needs. Depending so heavily upon a steady income flow unfortunately means that the sudden loss of a job can instantly spiral these families into dire financial straits from which they may take years to recover. Numerical comparisons reflect black wealth poverty as well.

For example, studies of wealth and net financial assets indicate that half of all white households possess nearly $7000 in net financial assets while roughly two-thirds of black families have either zero or negative net financial assets. Analyzing this data, one might be

---

30. *Id.* at 2.

tempted to conclude that the wealth disparity between whites and blacks is a function of the overall income disparity which is itself a function of the unequal access to employment opportunities. However, income differences explain only a portion of this disparate picture. Oliver & Shapiro discovered that when comparing blacks and whites making similar incomes, the wealth disparity remains, although the ratio becomes better as the income level increases. That is "[t]he highest earning black households possess twenty-three cents of median net financial assets for every dollar held by high-income white households." That is not the most critical part of the study, however, because the indicators also reveal that the lowest earning whites control almost as many net financial assets as the highest income blacks![31]

Certainly these numbers provide a rather shocking and sad commentary on the overall financial status of blacks in America. But the story doesn't end there because a summary of the data on wealth accumulation comparisons paints the most devastating picture of all: blacks control only 1.3% of the nation's financial asset pie, while whites control an astounding 95%. Moreover, this wealth accumulation inequality is likely to continue because even blacks who manage to acquire some degree of wealth typically amass consumable assets such as home and vehicle equity rather than long-term income producing assets like stocks and bonds.

So what is the overall impact of these decades of continued economic oppression and deprivation? Oliver & Shapiro summarized it as follows:

> The result was that generation after generation of blacks remained anchored to the lowest economic status in American society. The effect...has been to "sediment" this kind of inequality into the social structure. [Moreover], [j]ust as blacks have had "cumulative disadvantages," whites have had "cumulative advantages." Practically every circumstance of bias and discrimination against blacks has produced a circumstance and opportunity for positive gain for whites....The cumulative effect of such a process has been to sediment

---

31. *Id.* at 101.

blacks at the bottom of the social hierarchy and to artificially raise the relative position of some whites in society.[32]

This succinct yet accurate historical account of artificially constructed economic race relationships reveals quite clearly why many blacks in America are currently standing on the outside looking in as the digital economy transforms the way the world does business.

The Promise of the Internet and E-Commerce: Leveling the Playing Field?

The Internet and e-commerce show early promise as a playing field "leveler" where entrepreneurial ideas can be realized and wealth can be accumulated in the form of investment opportunities. Indeed, the e-commerce revolution holds particular promise for blacks because many of the traditional barriers to entrepreneurial success are either absent or minimized in the new digital economy.[33] For example, black entrepreneurs starting businesses in the physical world are often relegated to a primarily black clientele because the continuing legacy of racism effectively limits their access to white markets. E-commerce, which, in its simplest form, means conducting business on the Internet, offers access to local, state, national and international markets. Marketing products and services in the virtual world provides a degree of faceless anonymity that forces potential customers to focus on the quality of the product and/or service rather than the person promoting or selling the goods. In other words, if you build a professional website that provides quality prod-

---

32. *Id.* at 5.

33. Of course, not even the digital economy can remove all vestiges of discrimination and bias in the business and employment setting. For a sobering account of one black entrepreneur's struggles in the Internet economy, see Amy Harmon, *How Race is Lived In America: A Limited Partnership*, NEW YORK TIMES (New York), June 14, 2000.

ucts and excellent customer service, then, over time, customers and profits are likely to follow.

Of course, the key ingredient to initiating any new venture is financing. In the physical world, the venture capital process has traditionally been a roadblock to success for black entrepreneurs and, as a result, even the best laid business plans and visions have been thwarted by the lack of financial support. Can e-commerce help to equalize the flow of startup resources or venture capital to black entrepreneurs and businesses? Well, it's still a bit early in the e-commerce game to make such a determination, but it appears that the venture capital trend in e-commerce has been to fund workable *ideas*. In fact, the bulk of startup money for Internet and e-commerce ideas is generated from venture capital firms that are currently "chomping at the bit" to secure a stake in the digital economy. As proof that the Internet venture capital phenomenon has taken hold in the corporate world, in late 1999, several major American corporations announced plans to develop venture capital divisions within their companies. For example, Andersen Consulting reported that it would create a new venture capital division with the goal of investing approximately $1 billion over the next five years in Internet businesses. This announcement occurred during a year when overall venture capital financing in the United States increased nearly 150% to $35.6 billion, with more than half of that total going to fund Internet businesses. Such a dramatic shift in financial resources clearly signals a shift in the economy away from a manufacturing base and toward technology companies, with their potential for global sales and quick profits.

Much of the initial venture capital financing targeted business-to-consumer (B2C) e-commerce sites, i.e., Internet sites that provide some product or service directly to consumers. Many of these e-commerce sites resulted from average people working inordinately long hours to produce creative and workable ideas that attracted the attention of venture capital firms. Consider the example of Kozmo, an online company that caters to the public's demand for instant gratification by providing videos, snacks and electronics almost immediately after customers place orders online. Although the company has stumbled a bit recently, it is perhaps one of the best examples of the Internet's potential to help people realize their entrepreneurial dreams. The founder, a young Korean immigrant, conceived the idea for the company after he attempted to order a book online and discovered that he would have to wait several days for delivery. He found the experience extremely frustrating and thought there must be a better way to deliver goods to customers who want the instant gratification of shopping in the real world, but not the crowds and inconvenience. He immediately began making plans for his own Internet company based on this premise and realized his entrepreneurial dream when he and his college roommate launched Kozmo shortly thereafter. Initially, because the Kozmo co-founders were the only two employees of the company, they delivered products at night while seeking financing for the company during the day. Eventually, they obtained capital financing for the company and established Kozmo branches in six cities across the United States. It has been reported that since its inception, Kozmo has attracted $250 million in capital financing, including $60 million dollars from e-commerce giant, Amazon.com.

This is, of course, but one of the many e-commerce stories that demonstrate the entrepreneurial promise of the Internet. The skeptics among us might dismiss such examples as inapplicable to blacks, arguing that the same lack of financial support that has traditionally impeded the establishment of black businesses will also serve as a barrier to e-commerce endeavors. But, for the time being, that may not necessarily be the case. The digital revolution and the billions of venture capital dollars that support it appear ready to embrace minority entrepreneurs as well. For instance, the New York City Investment Corporation, which is financially backed by ten banks, supports minority ventures and has lent close to $1 million to two New York-based black-owned technology firms. Overall, it appears that at this early stage there is a recognition by many minority entrepreneurs that the e-commerce industry is still quite young and, so far, venture capital financing is colorblind. According to Keith Fulton, director of technology programs and policy at the National Urban League, "[t]he playing field is as level as it's going to get ... [y]ou don't need a $10 million marketing budget to put up a Website."[34] Fulton warns, how-

---

34. Janet Stites, *Prospectus: Black Entrepreneurs Spread the Word About "Digital Freedom,"* NEW YORK TIMES (New York), February 22, 1999.

ever, that other barriers to entry might emerge later due to the current consolidation in the e-commerce industry. By this statement, Fulton implies that getting into the e-commerce market early will allow minority entrepreneurs to take advantage of both the novelty of the industry and the relatively low-cost of entry. Those who come along later will find that the digital landscape has been whittled down to a few big players who have secured the bulk of the market share in any given industry, thus making it cost prohibitive for new players *of any color* to enter the market.

Corporate advertisers have also recognized the potential untapped markets available in the online environment as more and more minorities log on to the Internet. In an attempt to gain access to these markets, corporations are willing to financially support minority websites and portals. For example, Microsoft Corporation, USA Networks, the News Corporation, and Liberty Media contributed $35 million to BET.com, a website aimed primarily at blacks. BET.com hopes to take advantage of the increasing numbers of blacks going "digital" by providing a place to build community online. The site offers visitors the opportunity to chat virtually with others about a wide variety of topics and sells merchandise designed to appeal to minority audiences. In time, the web site also expects to serve as a convenient outlet for minority entrepreneurs to market their wares to global audiences.

The expanding technological landscape also increases opportunities for minorities in the employment context. Of course, the majority of the new jobs created by the e-commerce industry require some level of technology skills training and preparation. But once these skills are acquired, the employment opportunities are practically unlimited. Such technology training presents a viable career option for those mired in low-paying, dead-end jobs because, once trained, most technology workers can demand premium salaries and/or offer their services as independent consultants. Additionally, because certain technology occupations require only the use of a computer, modem and talent, some technology employees are able to telecommute, which means they can take advantage of the flexibility and convenience of working from any location where they can be "plugged in."

Employment in the technology field can also yield many intangible benefits not easily found in the "real world" work environment. For example, there is the unique sense of having control over one's destiny in a rapidly developing field with unlimited growth potential. While this sentiment is likely missing from many jobs in various industries, because of lingering institutional racism, blacks are particularly likely to perceive a lack of control over their work environments and a hopelessness in terms of the potential for substantial progress. Although some jobs in the technology industry are fast-paced and subject to unreasonable deadlines, most who are lucky enough to work in this environment are struck by the amount of freedom and flexibility afforded them in these occupations. Moreover, because the market for technology services is so competitive, properly trained employees do not have to waste away in dead-end jobs because, at any given moment, a new opportunity is just a resume away. In many respects then, the digital employment market might be likened to a vast, uncharted territory with numerous career opportunities currently available for the taking.

Embarking on a technology career may be a welcome option for most people, but the advent of the digital economy may not be greeted with open arms by those who are "downsized" from current occupations as a result of technological advancement. For instance, some companies are now discovering that it is more economically feasible to move certain of their sales and customer service functions to the Internet. This retrenchment usually reduces the need for human beings who currently carry out such services for the company. This kind of reduction in force often disproportionately impacts low-paying customer service positions, which, in some industries, are disproportionately occupied by non-skilled minority workers. Unless this group of employees obtains the requisite technology skills to compete for newly created positions, they will be faced with a shrinking demand for their skill sets. Furthermore, even job positions that do not directly involve working in the technology field now require some familiarity with technology as a prerequisite for securing the positions. Thus, in many instances, familiarity and interaction with technology will be an unavoidable characteristic of the 21st century job market.

Another intangible benefit accruing to those working in the digital economy results from the relative anonymity of Internet interactions. Auriea Harvey, a black female website designer and Internet entrepreneur, first believed that being anonymous was important to ensure that people judged her based upon her work rather than race or gender. She now realizes that although people may not initially know she is black, once they find out, "it's just trivia." To have one's race be considered trivial or secondary to one's knowledge and skills represents the true meaning of equal opportunity.

Lastly, and perhaps most important, the Internet offers great potential as a medium for minorities to learn about financial planning and begin taking conscious steps toward wealth accumulation. The stock market, with its cryptic numbers, symbols and terminology, can present a challenge to the unsophisticated investor. Simply plowing through the vast amounts of information and deciphering the language usually requires the assistance of brokers or financial analysts and, of course, the corresponding fees that typically accompany those services. Additionally, the financial requirements for entry into the investment world have traditionally excluded those without significant resources, resulting in the stock market being primarily the playground of the wealthy or well-connected. The technology revolution has altered or eliminated many of the obstacles to stock market investment. The Internet now provides unprecedented access to the stock market through a number of trading web sites geared toward the new and unsophisticated investor. Web sites such as E*Trade and Ameritrade offer access to a tremendous amount of background and explanatory information to help get potential investors acclimated to the stock market. The sites also permit individuals to begin buying and selling stock with as little as a $500 initial investment.

Online investment represents a potentially significant opportunity for reducing the wealth accumulation disparity between blacks and whites. Oliver & Shapiro report that liquid financial assets such as stocks, bonds and mutual funds account for almost one-third of the asset package for white families while blacks hold only 13% of such assets in their wealth portfolios. Easier access to the means for accumulating wealth could reasonably be expected to translate into a more focused and considered approach to wealth accumulation. Additionally, to the extent that these trading web sites provide detailed information to help potential investors create both short and long term investment and wealth accumulation objectives, then they can assist families in thinking about and planning for a more financially secure future even if they are not yet prepared to participate in stock transactions on the Internet. In other words, for some individuals, the educational material presented in the virtual world can positively influence their non-virtual life choices.

Finally... A Word About Reparations

There is currently an effort by black civil rights activists, politicians and academics to seek reparations for black citizens for the significant economic harm imposed by slavery. The reparations movement essentially demands that the federal government deliver on its original promise to provide "forty acres and a mule" to newly emancipated slaves at the end of the Civil War. As might be expected, there are political and practical problems associated with making such a demand. On the political side, although the demand addresses a tangible harm to slaves and a continuing harm to their descendants, the white descendants of slave owners most likely feel generationally removed from that harm and therefore not liable for paying any debts owed by their ancestors. Moreover, even if whites feel a degree of responsibility for the egregious harm inflicted, a mere transfer of wealth from the government to black people very much resembles a continuation of the "something for nothing" welfare state that many white and black Americans currently find so objectionable.

The practical side of the reparations demand presents even more challenges for its proponents. Chief among these difficulties is how to accurately quantify the harm to slaves and their descendents in order to pay a fair compensation for that harm. Most agree that the original promise of forty acres and a mule is no longer desirable. The question then is: what form of compensation should reparations take? Cash payments? Tax incentives? Low-interest loans? Educational scholarships? And even if a payment vehicle could be agreed upon, how would the harm be quantified? How much of the current state of black America can be attributed to the dehumanizing legacy of slavery? Forty percent? Eighty percent?

Without drawing any specific conclusions about the viability of demands for black reparations, I would argue that the technology landscape is a new frontier where everyone currently has an opportunity to stake a claim to a piece of the virtual world. Taking advantage of the real opportunities for employment, entrepreneurship and wealth accumulation offered by the digital revolution gives black Americans an unprecedented opportunity to level the economic playing field and begin building a solid financial base for future generations. Thus, while it might be helpful to look back on promises long forgotten and demand that they be fulfilled, that should certainly not overshadow a concentrated focus on the present and future opportunities that are currently available for the taking in the digital economy.

Chapter 3

The Education Gap

Education is a companion which no misfortune can depress, no crime can destroy, no enemy can alienate, no despotism can enslave. At home a friend, abroad an introduction, in solitude a solace, and in society an ornament. It chastens vice, it guides virtue, it gives, at once, grace and government to genius. Without it, what is man? A splendid slave, a reasoning savage.

Joseph Addison, *The Spectator*
November 6, 1711

The United States Supreme Court opinion in the landmark decision of *Brown v. Board of Education* signaled the end of a system of legalized educational segregation that had resulted in inferior education for generations of black students.[1] Given the tension filled race relations environment, it was probably not surprising that the Court's order to desegregate was flouted and superficially complied with as state and local governments scrambled to maintain the status quo. What was so important to these jurisdictions that they would

---

1. Brown v. Board of Education, 347 U.S. 483 (1954). The Court explained in Brown that

> [Education] is a principal instrument in awakening the child to cultural values, in preparing him for later professional training, and in helping him to adjust normally to his environment. In these days, it is doubtful that any child may reasonably be expected to succeed in life if he is denied the opportunity of an education. Such an opportunity, where the state has undertaken to provide it, is a right which must be made available to all on equal terms. Brown, at 493.

contemptuously disregard an order of the United States Supreme Court? What were they seeking to hold on to so vigorously? This chapter will examine the history of education in the United States as it pertains to black Americans. As in other social and economic areas, history reveals that blacks have faced overwhelming obstacles in the quest to obtain equal educational opportunity. The roots of these impediments can, perhaps not surprisingly, be traced back to the dehumanizing institution of slavery and the original denial of educational opportunities to slaves. These educational disadvantages have resonated throughout history and, even today, relegate millions of black children to dramatically inferior school settings. Although the countless judicial and legislative efforts to equalize educational opportunity for black students have met with limited success, an infusion of computer technology into the modern classroom curriculum, while certainly not a cure-all, demonstrates genuine potential for providing black youth with the fundamental access to information that so enhances the overall learning process.

Before examining how the digital revolution has potential to transform the everyday classroom experience for millions of black students, it is helpful to first explore how the educational system arrived at its current state of severely underserving minority populations. At least for black citizens, that history of educational disadvantage begins with slavery.

The Legacy of Slavery. . . . Again

The slave codes of the ante-bellum South forbid any person, even the slavemaster, from teaching a slave to read and write or employing him as a typesetter in a printing office or giving him books or pamphlets. To enforce these restrictions, heavy fines were often levied against those who violated them. Although some masters ignored the law and permitted slaves to learn to read and teach others, it was exceedingly difficult for a typical slave to acquire any more than a minimal education, and most did not receive even that much. For obvious reasons, it was quite beneficial to slaveholders and slavery advocates to keep slaves in an uneducated status for fear that a little bit of education might go a long way toward encouraging rebellion.

At the end of the Civil War, masses of uneducated former slaves struggled to adapt to life outside the bonds of slavery for which they were socially, financially and educationally unprepared. The literate world rejected them for the most part and adhered to firmly established beliefs that slaves were innately inferior on every level to whites and thus unteachable. The meager jobs that were available cast the free slaves in much the same subservient roles they played prior to emancipation. Practically no one encouraged education as a means to escape low status occupations because this cut against the self-interest of those who depended upon the former slaves' ignorance for their daily needs. This meant that the four million blacks freed from slavery had neither a fundamental education nor the resources to achieve such an education.

Nevertheless, as Gil Kujovich explains in "Equal Opportunity in Higher Education and the Black Public College: The Era of Separate but Equal," the newly freed slaves were remarkably eager to learn and embraced opportunities that offered a chance to obtain an education.[2] In response to this demand for education, sympathetic missionary and church groups from the North flooded the South to provide the freedmen with their first real opportunity to learn. These efforts eventually led to the creation of private black institutions, which would produce the majority of black college graduates

---

2. Gil Kujovich, *Equal Opportunity in Higher Education and the Black Public College: The Era of Separate But Equal*, 72 MINNESOTA LAW REVIEW 29, 38 (1987). Typical of the comments on the freed slaves' desire for an education was this statement by a teacher for the Pennsylvania Freedmen's Relief Association:

> It is wonderful how a people who have been so long crushed to the earth, so imbruted as these have been...can have so great a desire for knowledge, and such a capability for attaining it. One cannot believe that the haughty Anglo-Saxon race, after centuries of such an experience as these people have had, would be very much superior to them. Robert Morris, READING, 'RITING, AND RECONSTRUCTION: THE EDUCATION OF FREEDMEN IN THE SOUTH, 1861–1870 10 (1976) (quoting Charlotte Forten).

for many years to come. On the public front, state legislatures funded black normal schools for the professional training of black teachers. The training of black teachers to educate the masses of blacks pleased both blacks and whites since whites were wary of having white teachers "disgrace" themselves by educating blacks and blacks looked upon teachers of their own race as a source of pride and insurance against the hostility that would likely present itself if white teachers were entrusted with their education.

Land grant colleges were the next rung on the somewhat shaky ladder of education for black Americans. Although land grant colleges were originally created to make college education available to working class whites, Congress eventually required that institutions receiving federal money make no distinction of color or race in the admission of students. Unfortunately, a loophole in this congressional edict allowed schools to comply with this requirement by establishing and maintaining separate colleges for white and black students as long as the funds were *equitably* divided. This initial support for separate but equal educational facilities for blacks and whites had both short and long term ramifications. In the short term, the discriminatory policy led to the creation of seventeen black land grant colleges in the South. These colleges, which provided training in agriculture, industry and science, were a boon to blacks seeking a broad-based education and provided a welcome alternative to the previously established normal schools, which focused primarily on teacher training. Over the long term, however, the acceptance and "normalization" of a separate but equal framework for purposes of educating the nation's blacks signaled the beginning of the downward spiral toward persistently inferior educational opportunities for black students at all levels.

Seventy Years of Stagnant Inequality

As Kujovich describes, after the establishment of black public colleges, the "curriculum took on a unique form tailored to the *special* educational needs of blacks and the *special* needs of a segregated society.[3] These colleges were drastically and intentionally underfunded, which limited curricular objectives and isolated the schools from the broader academic community. In fact, the government funding was so meager that students, in addition to studying, performed manual labor in the form of constructing the buildings and carrying out maintenance and janitorial duties. As might be expected, due to shoddy building equipment and consequently poor construction, after a period of years, the buildings would deteriorate and no effort was made to restore them. Inside the buildings, the fundamental teaching tools such as blackboards, chalk and lab equipment, were inadequate to meet the academic needs of the faculty and student populations. Quite naturally, this severely underfunded situation resulted in a wide disparity in valuation between black land grant colleges and their white counterparts. For example, in 1928, the average black public institution was valued at $700,000, while the average white institution exceeded $4.5 million.

With regard to actual classroom instruction, the underfunded status of the black public colleges had a dramatic impact on both short and long term institutional curricular objectives. For instance, it was difficult to establish major programs in the sciences because lab equipment was limited or non-existent. Not surprisingly, these constraints on the education of black citizens played nicely into the hands of those who adhered to the fundamental belief that blacks were intellectually inferior and completely uneducable. The core curricula, which strongly encouraged "manual and industrial training," was basically designed to protect and maintain the caste system that already relegated black citizens to the lowest tier in the social strata.[4] Moreover, in a blatant attempt to maintain the status quo

---

3. Kujovich, *Equal Opportunity in Higher Education*, at 45. Kujovich concludes that "[a]n assumption of black inferiority lay at the heart of the system of segregation. Earlier used to justify slavery, theories of black inferiority found acceptance in white academia...as support for a narrow conception of black education." *Id.* at 64.

4. In his preeminent study of racism and black disadvantage, Gunnar Myrdal wrote about the intentionally limited curriculum available to black students in these terms:

There is a clear tendency to avoid civics and other social sciences

across the spectrum of social classes, some states even discouraged blacks from pursuing training in manual and industrial labor for fear that the lowest class of whites would face competition from a skilled black population. It is clear then, at every turn, meaningful education for the masses of black people was intentionally sacrificed to protect the interests of whites and preserve the caste system.

Of course, in an era of educational progress, these deliberately discriminatory practices served to place blacks further and further behind even the poorest whites, who were at least able to take advantage of the resource-rich land grant public colleges. As the economy shifted gears from agriculture to industry, the profound inequality in the allocation of educational resources meant that blacks were extraordinarily ill-prepared to take part in the burgeoning industrial revolution. It is no understatement to say that this "widespread and long-lasting denial of equal educational opportunity shaped the future of black Americans."[5]

Thus, when contemplating current educational standards, achievements and employment outlooks as they relate to black Americans, it is critical to consider that, even as America enters the 21st century, it is still not very far removed as a nation from the overtly segregationist period in its educational history. Perhaps it is not at all surprising that the majority of black Americans continue to experience the identifiable impact of this dreadful episode in America's recent past. Indeed, when examining the public education system in the 1940s and trying to determine what progress had been made in terms of the

---

in the Southern Negro public schools.... [A] special effort is made to prevent Negroes from thinking about the duties and privileges of citizenship....Where white students are taught about the Constitution and the structure of governments, Negroes are given courses in "character building," by which is meant courtesy, humility, self-control, satisfaction with the poorer things in life.... The content of the courses for Negroes throughout the South...is molded by the caste system at every turn. GUNNAR MYRDAL, AN AMERICAN DILEMMA: THE NEGRO PROBLEM AND MODERN DEMOCRACY 949 (1944).

5. Kujovich, *Equal Opportunity in Higher Education*, at 45.

overall education of black citizens since the creation of the first black public college in the 1860s, it became clear that:

> After seventy years of separate but equal higher educa-
> tion... [t]he black system of higher education continued to
> be dominated by black land grant colleges that were gener-
> ally denied the protection, and therefore the benefits, of fed-
> eral legislation. At all black public colleges, expenditures fell
> far short of any standard of fairness or equity. Educational
> programs continued to reflect discrimination and inequal-
> ity. Technical and scientific training was available in only
> the most rudimentary form, if at all. Graduate and profes-
> sional programs, with the exception of teacher training, did
> not exist. Few of the faculty, who had been victims of dis-
> crimination in their own education, had been able to attain
> doctorate degrees. Most were paid significantly less than
> their white counterparts and all suffered from a lack of op-
> portunities for professional development.[6]

"At the Same Place and at the Same Time"

During this seventy year period, the victims of the separate but equal educational policy were not simply content with their lot and instituted frequent legal challenges to this system of enforced segregation in the public school system. Early on, the intended strategy of these challenges was to adopt a piecemeal approach and concentrate on forcing states to comply with the equal part of the separate but equal doctrine. The late U.S. Supreme Court Justice Thurgood Marshall coordinated some of these legal challenges during his time as chief legal officer for the NAACP. As journalist and author Carl Rowan recounts in his book, *Dream Makers, Dream Breakers*, Mar-

---

6. *Id.* at 99.

shall's ultimate goal was to "wipe out all the trappings of white supremacy."[7] According to Rowan, Marshall "hated the hypocrisy of white Americans talking about 'law and order' and 'the rule of law' when they tolerated a situation where 'the law' for black people was whatever the white man said it was."[8]

Marshall's attack on the separate and decidedly unequal educational system began with graduate and professional schools, where it was believed they would face the least resistance from whites. Although many of the segregationist states scrambled to "equalize" their facilities in response to Marshall's legal challenges, he would always insist that more had to be done. In frustration, state officials sought assistance from Congress by requesting help to finance regional plans to establish separate graduate and professional schools for blacks. Marshall responded to this plan by advising the Senate Judiciary Committee that "[n]either Congress nor anyone else can say that you can get equality of education in a segregated school. The Fourteenth Amendment requires equality. The only way to get equality is for two people to get the same thing, at the same place and at the same time."[9]

Marshall's all out attack on the separate but equal doctrine took root in the hearts and minds of black people across the United States, leading to various lawsuits and protests challenging the doctrine.[10] One of those cases involved Linda Brown, a seven-year old black girl in Topeka, Kansas. In 1950, Brown's father attempted to enroll her in the all-white elementary school, which was four blocks away from her home. Even though Brown lived in an integrated neighborhood and within walking distance of this school, her enrollment was denied and she was told that she had to attend the

---

7. CARL T. ROWAN, DREAM MAKERS, DREAM BREAKERS: THE WORLD OF JUSTICE THURGOOD MARSHALL 143 (1993).

8. *Id.*

9. *Id.* at 153.

10. Although these cases were ostensibly challenging the segregated school system, as Rowan points out, "[a]lmost no one in the land was so naïve as to think that these cases were simply attacks on the Jim Crow schools... [they were] clearly an assault on the 'southern way of life'... [and] an attack on the ingrained racial customs..." *Id.* at 185.

"Negro" school two miles away.[11] This required Brown to walk several blocks and then take a bus, which was often late. Rather than accept these conditions, Brown's parents filed suit against the school board in Topeka. Brown's court case was initially handled by a local NAACP attorney in Topeka, but as the case worked its way to the United States Supreme Court, Marshall and an impressive team of lawyers, anthropologists and sociologists became involved in what was to become one of the landmark decisions in constitutional history.[12]

In the case of *Brown v. Board of Education*, it was decided that Marshall and his legal team would neither argue for equal schools for blacks, nor would they settle for the continuance of the "separate but equal" doctrine. Instead, Marshall's team would attempt to convince the Supreme Court "that the Constitution of a democracy could never give license to the stigmatic injuries of insult and exclusion that were being imposed upon Negro school children" by forcibly separating them in educational facilities based solely upon race. Marshall's argument was a full frontal attack on the separate but equal doctrine.[13]

---

11. As Linda Brown recalled many years later:
   Both of my parents were extremely upset by the fact that I had to walk six blocks through a dangerous train yard to the bus stop... only to wait, sometimes up to a half hour in the rain or snow, for the school bus that took me and the other black children to "our school." Sometimes, I was just so cold that I cried all the way to the bus stop... and two or three times I just couldn't stand it, so I came back home. *Id.* at 183 (quoting Linda Brown).

12. In addition to its unprecedented attack on the separate but equal doctrine, the Brown case also became well known for psychologist Kenneth Clark's creative use of dolls to demonstrate that black children suffered a severe stigma as a result of the forced system of educational segregation. Clark's doll test involved showing black children between the ages of six and nine identical black and white dolls and asking them to choose which doll was the "nice" doll. Of sixteen children tested, ten selected the white doll as the "nice" doll, while eleven chose the black doll as the "bad" doll. Clark claimed that this outcome clearly demonstrated that discrimination, prejudice and segregation have a detrimental impact on a child's concept of his own self-esteem.

13. Rowan, DREAM MAKERS, at 190.

The core of Marshall's legal argument was based upon section one of the Fourteenth Amendment, which prohibits the states from abridging the privileges and immunities of U.S. citizens, depriving them of life, liberty or property without due process of law or denying equal protection of the laws. Marshall argued before the Supreme Court that this constitutional amendment was intended to prohibit the states from continuing a system of state-imposed racial distinctions. Yet, Marshall contended, separate but equal educational facilities did just that by imposing a badge of inferiority on black school children who were prohibited from attending school with white children. According to Marshall, this system stigmatized black children in myriad ways that could not be remedied by merely providing them with equal facilities. Marshall, speaking in plain language to the Supreme Court, argued:

> Why, of all the multitudinous groups of people in the country, [do] you have to single out the Negroes and give them this separate treatment? It can't be because of slavery in the past, because there are very few groups in this country that haven't had slavery some place back in the history of their groups. It can't be color, because there are Negroes as white as the drifted snow, with blue eyes, and they are just as segregated as the colored men. The only thing it can be is an inherent determination that the people who were formerly in slavery, regardless of anything else, shall be kept as near that stage as possible. And now is the time, we submit, that this Court should make clear that that is not what our Constitution stands for.[14]

In May of 1954, after a reargument of the case, the United States Supreme Court delivered its opinion in the case of *Brown v. Board of Education*. The Court squarely confronted the segregation issue and succinctly stated the question presented: Does segregation of children in public schools solely on the basis of race, even though the physical facilities and other "tangible" factors may be equal, deprive the children of the minority group of equal educational opportunities? The Court's answer to this question was an unqualified and

---

14. *Id.* at 195–6.

unanimous: "We believe that it does." The Court's opinion continued with a discussion of the impact of segregation in public education and observed:

> Segregation of white and colored children in public schools has a detrimental effect upon the colored children. The impact is greater when it has the sanction of law; for the policy of separating the races is usually interpreted as denoting the inferiority of the Negro group. A sense of inferiority affects the motivation of a child to learn. Segregation with the sanction of law, therefore, has a tendency to [retard] the educational and mental development of Negro children and to deprive them of some of the benefits they would receive in a racial[ly] integrated school system.[15]

In a sweeping statement, the Court concluded that the doctrine of "separate but equal" has no place in the field of education because separate educational facilities are inherently unequal. The *Brown* opinion was heralded as the deathblow to segregation in education and the precursor to total elimination of the Jim Crow dual society that perpetuated the oppression and dehumanization of black people. The Court would later call the parties together again to hear arguments on an implementation plan to desegregate public schools in accordance with the Court's order. Not surprisingly, attorneys who argued in favor of maintaining the segregated school system urged the Court to either backtrack on its order to desegregate or implement the process at the slowest pace possible. To support their racist positions, these advocates raised the specter of black school children spreading untold numbers of diseases to white school children and lowered academic standards because of the inferior aptitude of black students. Finally, when it appeared as if the Court was not going to be particularly sympathetic to their biased, ignorant viewpoints, advocates for the state brazenly told the Court that if the order to desegregate was implemented in certain counties, the schools would cease to operate before they would tolerate integration of the races. In fact, one advocate even went so far as to warn the Court that there would be open defiance to the desegregation

---

15. Brown, at 494.

order by declaring "in all candor and frankness to [the] Court, that solution whatever it may be, will not in my judgment in the lifetime of those of us hale and hearty here, be enforced integration of the races in the public schools...."[16] Despite these threats and dire predictions, the Court ordered the public schools to begin the process of desegregation. But, taking into account that the desegregation process required a wholesale upheaval of the established educational system in many states, the Court advised that in establishing an implementation plan, the lower courts could consider problems related to administration, physical condition of the school plant, the school transportation system, personnel, revision of school districts and attendance areas and revision of local laws and regulations. In its final decree, the Supreme Court ordered the lower courts to "take such proceedings and enter such orders and decrees consistent with [the *Brown* opinion] as are necessary and proper to admit to public schools on a racially nondiscriminatory basis *with all deliberate speed* the parties to these cases."[17]

The Aftermath of Brown

As history has revealed, what followed the Court's implementation order in the second *Brown* opinion was deliberate and speedy only in the sense that many states deliberately evaded the Court's order and were noticeably speedy in doing so. For example, some states introduced pupil placement and freedom of choice laws. A typical example of these statutes was the Alabama School Placement Law, which provided that students were to be assigned and transferred to schools based upon sixteen obscure factors. The factors included examining the potential for psychological distress associated with attendance at a particular school and the possibility of friction or disorder at the school. The law also permitted students to opt out of atten-

---

16. Rowan, DREAM MAKERS, at 232.
17. Brown v. Board of Education, 349 U.S. 294, 301 (1955).

dance at a school where the races were commingled upon written objection of a parent or guardian. The Supreme Court dealt harshly with many of these evasive tactics and in a series of post-*Brown* opinions once again ordered the public schools to desegregate.

Without minimizing the heroic efforts of those who fought the noble and just fight to desegregate public schools, the practical results of the *Brown* opinions have indeed brought mixed blessings to this country's black Americans. On the one hand, it was quite clear that the separate but equal system was devastatingly stigmatizing to black students, and therefore, it was critical that these students gain full access to the same educational opportunities as white students in order to have a chance to succeed in life. On the other hand, it appears that while the *psychological* impact of the separate but equal system was explored with the help of Kenneth Clark's doll experiments, very little attention was paid to the psychological toll that could be visited upon black students once they were legally within the classrooms of formerly all-white institutions. As is so often the case with fundamental changes in the law, societal attitudes and behavior are not swept away quite as dramatically. In fact, some of the black students who were part of the early desegregation plans described their circumstances as "going to war" everyday. In that kind of bitter and chaotic environment, one could hardly expect that there was much in terms of education taking place. It might also be reasonably presumed that deep-seated hostile attitudes and biased perceptions concerning black students would be manifest at every level, including the teachers, who were now charged with educating in a multiracial environment.

Perceptual Inequality

Without regard to what the law mandated in *Brown v. Board of Education*, preconceived notions about the learning abilities of black children, rooted in a legacy of slavery and IQ pseudoscience, often determined the extent of education black students received in the post-*Brown* classroom. In his article, *Teachers' Perceptions and Expec-*

tations and the Black-White Test Score Gap, Ronald Ferguson summed up the perceptual phenomenon in this way: "Consider people who learn from real life that when one flips a coin the odds of getting heads are 60:40. Place these people in an experimental situation where, unknown to them, the odds have been set to 50:50. If each person is then given only one toss of the coin, will their predictions be unbiased?"[18] Various studies have shown that these preconceived ideas influence teachers' estimation of students' full potential in the sense that teachers are likely to consistently underestimate the potential of black children. For example,

> in the middle class white school, student inattention was taken as an indication of teacher need to arouse student interest, but the same behavior in a lower class black school was rationalized as boredom due to limited student attention span. In general, the teachers in the lower class black school were characterized by low expectations for the children and low respect for their ability to learn.[19]

Of course, low expectations can result in self-fulfilling prophecies, particularly if those attitudes are somehow communicated to children. Often, the children will respond by not trying as hard because they perceive their efforts as an exercise in futility given the teachers' attitude toward them. Quite simply, students become disengaged from the learning process. Disengaged students are then categorized and tracked into special classes or a less academically demanding, non-college preparatory curricula, which ultimately narrows their perceptions and long-term opportunities. This manner of tracking students by perceived ability also helps to recreate the system of racial inequality in the classroom, thereby producing the irony of inequality and resegregation in a nominally equal educational opportunity setting. Not only do these biased perceptions and categorizations impact students who are tracked, they can also make black students who are capable of achieving acutely aware that they are in

---

18. Ronald F. Ferguson, *Teachers' Perceptions and Expectations and the Black-White Test Score Gap*, in THE BLACK-WHITE TEST SCORE GAP 273, at 277 (Christopher Jencks & Meredith Phillips eds., 1998).
    19. *Id.* at 281.

a racial fishbowl, constantly being measured against stereotyped assessments of black academic achievement.

Claude Steele and Joshua Aronson have discussed the profound effect negative stereotypes can have on the achievement levels of even *academically successful* black students. In their article, *Stereotype Threat and the Test Performance of Academically Successful African Americans*, Steele and Aronson argue that "African American students know that any faltering could cause them to be seen through the lens of a negative racial stereotype. Those whose self-regard is predicated on high achievement—usually the stronger, more confident students—may feel this pressure so greatly that it disrupts and undermines their test performance."[20] Accordingly, those black students who are most determined to achieve academically are likely to underperform due to excessive concern about unintentionally confirming a negative stereotype regarding black intellectual capabilities. Indeed, as Steele & Aronson posit, this negative stereotype threat can be so pervasive that it can be triggered by describing a test as a measure of ability or merely asking blacks to indicate their race on a test form.

Finally, and perhaps most important, Phillip J. Cook and Jens Ludwig assert in their paper, *The Burden of 'Acting White': Do Black Adolescents Disparage Academic Achievement*, that black-white differences in academic achievement may be partially the result of black students' internalized doubt about their own intellectual ability and a corresponding acceptance of educational advancement as the "white" thing to do.[21] Unable to reconcile these negative doubts, some black students begin to subtly and sometimes not so subtly attempt to persuade their peers against academic achievement by categorizing them as "acting white." Noted education scholar John Ogbu refers to this peer pressure dynamic as "cultural inversion" and describes it as "a process whereby subordinate group members come to

---

20. Claude M. Steele & Joshua Aronson, *Stereotype Threat and the Test Performance of Academically Successful African Americans*, in THE BLACK-WHITE TEST SCORE GAP 401, at 402 (Christopher Jencks & Meredith Phillips eds., 1998).

21. Philip J. Cook & Jens Ludwig, *The Burden of "Acting White": Do Black Adolescents Disparage Academic Achievement?* in THE BLACK-WHITE TEST SCORE GAP 375 (Christopher Jencks & Meredith Phillips eds., 1998).

define certain forms of behaviors, events, symbols, and meanings as inappropriate for them because these are characteristics of their oppressors...."[22] Conduct by blacks that is typically regarded as "acting white" includes performing well academically and advancing in high-status jobs in the mainstream economy. Blacks who dare to engage in this achievement-oriented behavior are labeled as "Uncle Toms" and "oreos." Essentially then, one's racial identity is held hostage and the ransom demands are outright rejection of all that is considered "white," including educational advancement—a hefty price to pay indeed.

Much of the social and psychological analysis of the post-*Brown* classroom indicates that black students have not fared nearly as well as the proponents of educational equality might have hoped. This is not meant to imply that the continuing struggle for equal educational opportunity is futile because certainly there has been some progress and Americans witness the tangible results of this everyday with the increase in black lawyers, doctors, and business professionals. However, attitudes regarding the inferior status of blacks that flow directly from the legacy of slavery are more enduring and pernicious than many who fought the good fight could have imagined. In addition, the desegregation plans and court orders that were hammered out in the wake of the *Brown* decisions now face constant legal challenges to their continued necessity as school districts proudly boast that they have reached a unitary state and are therefore no longer obligated to desegregate. This so-called unitary state masks the harsh reality that many of these school systems have become predominantly black and suffer the same financial and resource difficulties as the separate but equal schools of the pre-*Brown* era. Although a number of social and economic factors combined to produce this result, the chief cause was a phenomenon known as "white flight." That is, rather than comply with the Supreme Court's order to desegregate, many whites simply chose to leave the school district altogether. This mass abandonment of central cities more

---

22. John Ogbu, *Opportunity Structure, Cultural Boundaries, and Literacy,* in Language, Literacy, and Culture: Issues of Society and Schooling 154 (Judith Langer ed., 1987).

often than not resulted in a diminished tax base for schools to draw upon as a resource. Without this essential source of revenue, inner-city public schools have once again fallen into disrepair and financial resources within these school systems are spread too thinly to adequately educate the largely minority student populations. Confronted with minimal resources, low academic achievement and widespread discipline problems, many teachers forced to educate in these dismal surroundings have come to regard their roles not as educators but as wardens who simply confine and control the student population for a given period of time during each school day.

Of course, dire financial circumstances do not excuse the duty to educate black youth. But one can certainly sympathize with the enormous hurdles and challenges that teachers and administrators face in these situations, particularly when courts and legislatures have turned a deaf ear to further demands for desegregation and increased financial resources. In the face of diminishing tax bases and deteriorating infrastructures, a focus on acquiring and integrating computer technology into the curriculum may seem, at best, impractical. However, as the next section will explore, these resources may indeed provide much needed expansion of access to information and development of critical technology skills that will prepare students for the future despite their surroundings.

Classrooms Without Walls: A Digital Promise of Equality?

As I have discussed in an earlier article on the desegregation dilemma, there are two possible responses to the current trend toward resegregation and the courts' retreat from the desegregation plans adopted after the *Brown* case.[23] One response is to continue a

---

23. Raneta J. Lawson, *The Child Seated Next to Me: The Continuing Quest for Equal Educational Opportunity*, 16 THURGOOD MARSHALL LAW REVIEW 35, 48–54 (1990).

pattern of litigation designed to force further desegregation of schools that have become resegregated due to white flight. The success of this option would depend upon the courts' willingness to become more practical and flexible when defining neighborhoods in order to account for various demographic shifts when designing effective desegregation remedies. However, even if courts are amenable to such creative remedies, these kinds of expanded desegregation plans have inherent limitations. For example, William Raspberry described a situation in Prince George's County, an area near the District of Columbia, where a large number of whites left the public schools, moving farther out of the county, while more blacks moved into the county. Over time, the public school system, which had been 13% black, became more than 40% black. Raspberry observed that in such a setting, not only would continued litigation likely result in more white flight but may lead to the "absurd phenomenon of black children traveling great distances from their neighborhood only to wind up in schools that are overwhelmingly black." As Raspberry further explained, forcing black children to travel needless miles in order to sit next to white children is not only wasteful, but addresses the wrong problem because "color isn't the problem; education is."[24]

A second possible rejoinder to the resegregation dilemma is to focus on educating black children regardless of environment. Much like the focus on litigation, this solution will also require creative and flexible thinking. However, rather than wasting scarce resources on costly litigation, this remedy seeks to maximize available resources, with a principal focus on cultivating *human* resources. It appears that somehow in the midst of the post-*Brown* haste to desegregate, an attitude developed that white schools were superior and were the *only* places where black children could acquire an education. But, as some of the post-*Brown* teacher perception studies reveal, learning is most often a function of attitude and when administrators and teachers perceive children as educable without regard to race and environment, then learning can take place even in the face

---

24. William Raspberry, *Why is Busing the Only Route?* WASHINGTON POST, September 4, 1981, at 29.

of minimal resources. Quite naturally, the kinds of resources available will determine the extent of a child's education. That is, even with the most committed teachers, black students are likely to be less prepared academically if they are learning from outdated textbooks. Here is where the promise of technology can expand the classroom and create a global learning environment for children.

A recent report by the Department of Education describing the Universal Service Fund for Schools and Libraries (commonly known as E-Rate), found that:

During the past 20 years, the role of the computer in American schools has expanded as its capacity as a learning tool has changed, and it has increasingly become an integral part of daily classroom life. In particular, the Internet has exposed students to topics that they could previously only find in textbooks or at the library, has enabled teachers to enrich their classroom instruction, has provided increased opportunities for teacher professional development (e.g., through distance learning), and increased the efficiency of routine administrative tasks (e.g., recording grades).... [Moreover], the Internet can allow students to learn outside the regular classroom, expand educational opportunities for rural and other isolated students, and allow educators to communicate with their colleagues in the United States and around the world. Students, with "the click of a button," can find and explore information that once would have required extensive library research, or may have been totally unavailable to them in their school or local library.[25]

This broad statement summarizes the expectations and potential of computer technology and the Internet in the classroom environment. According to the E-Rate Study, "[i]n this new view of education, computers are no longer necessarily seen as a supplement to the classroom (i.e., reinforcing what is taught by the teacher), but the foundation around which teaching and learning can take

---

25. MICHAEL J. PUMA, ET AL., THE URBAN INSTITUTE, E-RATE AND THE DIGITAL DIVIDE: A PRELIMINARY ANALYSIS FROM THE INTEGRATED STUDIES OF EDUCATIONAL TECHNOLOGY (2000) 4–6.

place."[26] In terms of what technology can mean for students, the E-Rate Study discusses two separate studies that examined the impact of computer technology in rural and low-income classrooms. One study discovered that in very disadvantaged schools, technology enhanced student motivation and learning. Similarly, the second study determined that the use of technology improved students' basic math and reading skills and resulted in small positive increases in test scores, particularly for rural and low-income children.[27]

Although computer technology is an essential component of the 21st century classroom, the E-Rate Study acknowledges that current efforts to integrate technology in the classroom are limited by the same socioeconomic realities that have played a role in creating impoverished school systems. That is, while all public schools are equally likely to have Internet access *in at least one room*, getting access at the classroom level where it can be incorporated into daily instruction has been more of a challenge. As might be expected, the percentage of classrooms with access is divided along wealth lines, with 74 percent of the wealthiest schools likely to have classroom access while only 39 percent of the poorest schools have similar capabilities.[28]

To help bridge this educational technology gap, in 1996, the Clinton administration announced four National Technology Goals in the area of education and technology. The goals are:

- Teachers will have the training and support needed to help students use computers and the Internet to learn
- Classrooms will have modern multimedia computers
- Classrooms will be connected to the Internet
- School curricula will use software and online learning to ensure that no child is left behind

To meet these goals, the Department of Education developed several technology initiatives aimed at increasing the effective use of technology in the nation's elementary and secondary schools. One

---

26. *Id.* at 5.
27. *Id.* at 12–13.
28. *Id.* at 7.

program, the Technology Literacy Challenge Fund, represents the Department's single largest financial investment in helping schools embrace technology, with a special emphasis on communities with high concentrations of poor children. In 1997, the Fund received $200 million in allocations, which was given to the states to distribute to local school districts.

Another significant program designed to equalize access to technology is the E-Rate program. Authorized by the Telecommunications Act of 1996, E-Rate "provides all public and private schools and libraries...access to affordable telecommunications and advanced digital technologies."[29] The overall objective of the program is to assist schools with limited budgets to acquire these services at reduced rates, thereby allowing them to redirect scarce resources into other related activities such as the professional development of teachers and acquisition of computer hardware and software. The E-Rate program allows eligible schools and libraries to receive discounts ranging from 20 to 90 percent, depending upon economic need and location (urban or rural). These discounts are available on eligible telecommunications services, which includes basic local and long distance telephone services, Internet access, and the acquisition and installation of equipment to provide network wiring within school and library buildings. Although computer hardware and software are not included in the program, as noted above, the hope is that schools will utilize the extra savings afforded by the E-Rate program to fund these acquisitions.

Because acquiring computer technology and services is only the first step toward establishing a digital classroom, the E-Rate program application requires schools and libraries to develop a detailed plan to integrate technology into the curriculum once the equipment and services are installed. For example, the E-Rate application must address how the school or library staff will learn to use networked information technologies for improved education or library services. In addition, schools must certify that they have funds budgeted and approved to meet the financial obligations associated with the "non-discounted" portion of their requested services. Although the E-Rate

---

29. *Id.* at 19.

program was initially quite controversial, it has maintained solid support and provided $1.7 billion in its first year of operation and approximately $2.4 billion in its second year.[30] To date, research on the effectiveness of the E-Rate program has determined that the discounts have, in fact, allowed school districts to achieve faster deployment of computer networks and Internet access and reinvest the savings in other important technology needs.[31]

When examining the overall goal of the E-Rate program to assist schools in low-income communities and rural areas obtain technology services, initial data on fund distribution indicate that indeed the program is achieving that objective. In the first year of operation, the most severely impoverished school districts had somewhat lower application rates than might have been expected. This anomaly was believed to be due to limited knowledge of the program coupled with limited funds to allocate for technology infrastructure not covered by the E-Rate funds (a prerequisite for participation in the program). However, in the second year of the program, the application rate for this category of schools rose, indicating that the program was indeed gaining further penetration of its target market. Moreover, in terms of real dollars allocated to minority students, more than $800 million have been committed to districts with 50 percent or more minority students.

Nevertheless, even as it makes strides toward narrowing the digital divide in the classroom, the E-Rate program may still be unable to reach some of the nation's smallest and poorest schools. Critics of the program contend that the bureaucratic requirements and mandatory financial outlays make it impossible for some schools to participate in the program even if they are given a 90 percent dis-

---

30. The controversy stemmed from the claim by some telephone companies that E-Rate represented an illegal tax on their industry because they were required to pay into the Universal Service Fund (which funds E-Rate), while Internet Service Providers were not required to make such payments.

31. The program is not without its glitches, however, and some E-Rate program participants have encountered difficulty in obtaining the necessary technology infrastructure that is not covered by the E-Rate fund, thereby limiting their ability to take full advantage of the resources provided by the E-Rate program.

count on the services covered by the E-Rate program. In some cases, it's simply a matter of not having the necessary staff to gather the information required for the detailed application process. For others, amassing the 10 percent co-pay constitutes an excessive financial burden when coupled with the outlays required to update their infrastructures to take advantage of the technology. It is hoped that states will eventually make financial commitments to fill the void for the most poverty stricken school districts in order to ensure that no child is left behind in the digital revolution.

Corporations have also offered technology assistance and training to help bring poor school districts into the digital age. For instance, Microsoft targeted low-income school districts with the message that they can save money and time by implementing an integrated Microsoft software system.[32] In one case, the Houston Independent School District, which is largely urban and populated by a disproportionate number of disadvantaged students, decided that despite its limited resources it was obligated to take steps to prepare students for the high technology workplace. The school district accomplished this goal by implementing an integrated Microsoft system and, as a result, the district is now leading the state and the country in technology usage. The district now boasts 12,500 personal computers, with more than three-quarters of these connected to a network. This nearly universal connectivity allows students to use the Internet for instructional purposes and increases the efficiency of teachers and administrators, who can now communicate with each other and access important student information with the click of a button.

The Houston example illustrates that not only is it critical to acquire technology, but it is equally important to discover ways to seamlessly integrate that technology into business operations so that it does not become a practical burden. In other words, schools must avoid jumping on the bandwagon and acquiring technology solely for the sake of owning technology. Additionally, educators must be cognizant of the fact that they are also likely to face challenges to technology implementation from *outside* the classroom. As dis-

---

32. As might be expected, corporate largess is often inextricably linked with a profit motive.

cussed in Chapters 1 and 2 of this book, a fear of science and technology may hinder some students from immediately embracing technology. Furthermore, a lack of financial resources at home may preclude some from purchasing personal computers to assist in research and other class assignments during non-classroom hours. Thus, like most intractable social issues, the problem of integrating technology into minority school district classrooms is multi-faceted and will not be resolved by simply throwing dollars at the issue.

This raises one concern regarding the implementation of technology in classrooms that has become quite controversial. That is, some educators and policy analysts are simply not convinced that having more computers in the classroom will yield greater educational achievements. Groups such as the Alliance for Childhood contend that, among other things, computers pose serious health hazards to children. Physical injuries such as eyestrain and psychological damage from social isolation are among the concerns that the group raises when considering the current emphasis on technology in the classroom. Arguing that school reform is a social challenge, not a technological problem, the Alliance points to a 1999 study by the Department of Education that describes the transformation of nine troubled schools in high-poverty areas, "all places resigned to low expectations, low achievement and high conflict...." The schools became "high-achieving, cohesive communities [when] everyone involved—principals, teachers, other staff members, parents, and students—developed high expectations of themselves, and of each other." The report concluded that:

> The strategies that worked in these schools were persistence, creativity in devising new ways of collaborating, maximizing the attention focused on each child, and a shared commitment to meeting the full range of children's needs. That intensely human approach—not large expenditures on technology—is what seems to have moved all nine communities from despair to hope. Educational technology plays only a relatively minor role in the report.

Indeed, the human approach is without question the most fundamental component of educational reform for low-income minority communities. For too long, it seems that children have been treated as pawns in a numbers game as school districts endeavor to maintain a delicate balance in the racial make-up of schools. At some point in the process, education took a backseat to headcounts and statistics. Admittedly, some progress toward equal educational opportunity has been made, but much more is necessary. Further efforts at educational reform must, however, keep an eye toward the future. In today's electronic age, children who are unfamiliar with technology face an uncertain employment outlook and a diminished capacity for significant economic progress. Technology can and should be incorporated into the modern school curriculum and used as a tool for *enhancing* the learning process. But perhaps more importantly, the use of technology in the classroom also begins the process of orientation toward the digital landscape. Thus, the creation of classrooms without walls through the use of technology can open a child's world and expand its boundaries beyond the realities of poverty stricken communities. And sometimes being able to *see* beyond one's immediate environment is all that is necessary to capture the imagination and encourage the thirst for learning.

PART II

THE IMPACT OF THE DIGITAL DIVIDE

Chapter 4

Communication and Networking

The Internet infrastructure is a global interconnection of computer systems that enables the virtually effortless exchange of information without regard to geographical boundaries. Despite its current widespread public appeal, the Internet began primarily as a means for academics and researchers to overcome the limitations of traditional communication processes and correspond with colleagues quickly across long distances. Today, although the Internet is used for a variety of other purposes, it continues to provide a convenient and efficient method for people to connect across local, national and global boundaries. Just as in "real life," communication on the Internet occurs on a variety of levels with many different expectations and goals. Some virtual communication tools, such as e-mail, chat groups, bulletin boards and instant messaging, are useful for everyday exchanges between relatives and friends, and today, are increasingly being implemented in business environments to speed information exchange and reduce the amount of excess paper. As might be expected, rapid paperless information exchange in today's multi-national business milieu is particularly convenient and cost-effective because it facilitates correspondence across long distances. This means, for example, that corporate offices in the United States can communicate with their overseas subsidiaries and receive responses in a matter of minutes via e-mail.

This chapter will explore the various communication tools currently available on the Internet and through other forms of computer technology. Because an increasing amount of the world's personal and business communication is taking place through virtual media, those who do not take advantage of these modern means of communication will not only forego the potential efficiencies associated with these new avenues, but will almost certainly find themselves outside the flow of critical information that so often enables many in our high technology society to get ahead.

Some may initially wonder exactly how technology communication tools are essential to narrowing the digital divide. After all, technology is but one means of interaction in a society that has numerous other communication options ranging from shouting across the neighbor's fence to placing a long distance telephone call. First, the distinction between the haves and have nots in the digital divide is not simply a matter of who is capable of affording or accessing the relevant computer hardware and software technology. The digital divide also concerns who has *access to the fundamental information channels* that are a critical component of this new technology medium. Millions of bytes of information flow across Internet information channels everyday. Much like one might find in real life by sitting idly on a busy street corner and listening to the conversations of passersby, some of this virtual communication is nonsensical, some of it mundane, some of it uplifting, some of it intelligent and some of it conducive to income producing opportunities. But unlike the busy street corner where passersby would probably not expect or welcome the participation of strangers in their conversational exchanges, the Internet encourages a unique kind of community building where spontaneous participation in the global exchange of information is both expected and welcomed. In this mélange of exchanges, relationships are formed, families are connected, learning takes place, and business deals are struck. To put it simply, in the digital age, access to these information channels confers advantage while non-access yields tremendous disadvantage. So whether the communication involves planning the semi-annual family reunion, grandma sending an e-birthday card to her granddaughter, or an inner-city high school student participating in a chat room discussion with other teens across the country about a difficult algebra problem, the Internet is fast becoming the preferred method for easily connecting with others across boundaries to communicate, learn and expand opportunities.

E-Mail

It is estimated that millions of e-mail messages are sent and received each day, making it the most widely used communication tool in the Internet environment. The widespread use of e-mail is probably not surprising given the ease with which this technology may be located, learned and utilized. Indeed, e-mail is often the first introduction to online technology for many computer novices. In its simplest form, acquiring and using an e-mail account doesn't even require owning a personal computer. An e-mail account may be obtained from one of the many free e-mail web sites on the Internet such as Hotmail, Yahoo or Excite. Sites offering free e-mail accounts are generally secure, which minimizes the concern that others will gain unauthorized access to private e-mail communications. Since these accounts are Internet based, they also offer the convenience of accessibility from any computer terminal attached to the Internet. Thus, users can access their e-mail from anywhere in the world. Moreover, those who don't have access to computers at home may also take advantage of this communication tool by establishing and accessing free e-mail accounts at numerous public and private locations that provide Internet access to the public.[1]

Another popular method for establishing and utilizing e-mail is securing a personal Internet access account with a specific Internet Service Provider (ISP). Users may then choose to establish an e-mail account (or several e-mail accounts) with their ISP, which permits them to send and receive e-mail across the ISP's networks. Typically, these types of e-mail accounts must be accessed by dialing into the ISP's network, and therefore, access away from home may be limited.[2]

---

1. For instance, many employees who don't have computers at home access the Internet from work and establish e-mail accounts. This allows them to conveniently stay in touch with friends and relatives while also acquiring a modicum of information about how computer technology works. The downside for many employers, of course, is that too much Internet and e-mail use in the workplace usually translates into decreased productivity.

2. However, recognizing the convenience of accessing e-mail anytime and anywhere, many ISPs are beginning to make their e-mail accounts accessible through the Internet.

Employers and universities also routinely provide employees and students with e-mail accounts. Today, in the modern business context, memos and voice mail are often replaced by e-mail as the means of choice for fast, reliable inter- and intra- office communication. As mentioned previously, e-mail provides the unique ability to quickly link far flung branches of a corporation together with the click of a button. Global communications that previously took hours or days to accomplish are now completed in a fraction of that time. Because corporate networks and e-mail have become valuable tools for conducting business, e-mail accounts in the corporate setting are usually restricted to business-related communications. Despite these restrictions, however, employees are notorious for routinely sending personal e-mail across the corporate network, which can lead to a variety of disastrous results for the companies involved.

For instance, the entire corporate network may be disabled if a computer virus is introduced into the system. Computer viruses usually enter networks via e-mail accounts when users open e-mail attachments that contain the viruses. Once introduced, the virus is then spread effortlessly from user to user as it propagates itself throughout the network, sometimes managing to overwhelm the system with the sheer number of e-mails produced by the virus. In early 2000, many corporations were caught off guard by a notorious computer bug known as the ILOVEYOU virus. The virus arrived as a seemingly harmless e-mail with the subject line "ILOVEYOU" and an attachment that purported to be a love letter from the sender. However, as soon as the attachment was opened, the virus was activated and immediately sent itself to everyone in the user's e-mail address book. Hundreds of corporations were crippled for several days as the e-mail virus inundated corporate networks and prevented the transmission of normal business-related e-mail communications.

Another hazard of ignoring the business-related e-mail restriction concerns communications over the corporate network that contain offensive or inflammatory material, which can result in liability for the corporation if such communications are not adequately policed by corporate management. What this means is that, at minimum, corporations must institute policies that forbid non-business related communications over the corporate network and take steps to ensure maximum compliance with this prohibition. Additionally, and perhaps most important for the corporation, such policies must be promptly enforced against employees who disregard the restrictions and continue to use e-mail accounts at work to send any manner of personal correspondence.

Finally, sending personal e-mail over a corporate network implicates significant privacy issues for employees. In the typical corporate setting, all of the computer hardware, software, and network connections are the property of the employer and remain so even though employees are allowed to use the equipment for work-related tasks. Occasionally, employees may develop a false sense of security and privacy with respect to e-mail communications in the workplace engendered by the fact that computers are located in their private workspaces and access to the network requires the use of a self-selected password. In other words, proximity and personal passwords may enhance a feeling of personal ownership and privacy in the computer equipment. Nothing could be further from the truth however. Despite the location of the computer and the password system, computer hardware, software and network systems are owned by the company. Consequently, any communication that travels across the network is subject to interception and viewing by corporate officials at any time. In fact, it behooves companies to periodically inspect e-mail traffic flowing across their networks to ensure that employees are adhering to the business-related e-mail standards.

In the university setting, students are typically given access to the university's network resources, including e-mail, web pages and the Internet. On many university campuses, to gain access to the university's network, students must pay a technology fee and agree not to abuse their privileges while using the network. However, just as in the corporate environment, access and usage restrictions are routinely ignored and violators generally face sanctions by university administration including expulsion from the university.

With the variety of options available for establishing e-mail accounts, it is perhaps not surprising that millions of people use this communication tool everyday, even some users who don't know or care to know anything else about Internet technology. Undoubtedly, the lure of e-mail is attributable to its ease of access and obvious relevance to the lives of those who value its convenient and instantaneous nature. Users can communicate with friends and relatives across miles with little or no delay and receive a response within minutes if the recipient happens to be online at the time. In fact, many attribute the decline in personal letter writing to the advent of e-mail. Also, in many cases, because the cost of sending e-mail is low in comparison to long distance phone calls (especially if the call is international), users can realize a significant cost savings without losing much in the way of efficient and effective communication.

Of course, technically speaking, e-mail does not offer the same level of privacy that one would likely receive from sending a personal letter or making a telephone call. Although most e-mail account providers guarantee *relatively* secure communications, it is important to remember that this assurance is quite limited in the Internet environment. Indeed, sending an e-mail has often been analogized to sending a postcard through the U.S. Post Office system. Just as anyone who handles the postcard can potentially read its contents, any computer network that receives and transmits an e-mail communication can intercept that communication and expose its contents to view by unauthorized persons. This is because an e-mail transmitted by a sender to a recipient rarely travels directly to that person. Instead, depending upon network traffic, the e-mail may travel across a variety of networks before reaching its final destination. Although the chances are slim that any given e-mail communication will be intercepted, it is generally inadvisable to send any information across an e-mail system that one would not place on a postcard.

With its multiple uses, e-mail has in many ways brought the world closer together. Indeed, those who study technology trends have discovered that, in some instances, e-mail has resulted in deeper and more personal communications because people feel more freedom to openly express themselves through the written word. E-mail technology has also had a remarkable impact in the educational environment by helping to bring the classroom closer to those who, because of life circumstances, are not able to fully participate in the traditional classroom setting.

For example, the Kentucky Migrant Technology Project uses e-mail as part of an overall technology program to serve the needs of migrant workers/students in rural Kentucky. Approximately 20,000 migrant students reside in Kentucky, making it one of the top ten populated migrant areas in the United States.[3] Such a large migrant student population creates myriad problems for educators including "low academic achievement... and the lack of continuity of education among these students moving from one location to another."[4] One of the goals of the migrant technology program is to increase continuity of education by bringing the classroom to students who cannot attend classes regularly due to their mobile existence. In keeping with this mission, "the Migrant Technology Project has addressed the problem of low academic achievement among migrant students by utilizing technology to provide a highly motivational, multi-media based curriculum that is specifically adapted to cultural, educational, and language needs of the students."[5] Using community access centers that are specially equipped with technology for the migrant students' use, students can keep up with assignments and e-mail homework if they are unable to attend classes. Additionally, to facilitate mobile connectivity, some students are issued personal digital assistants (PDAs) or mobile communication devices that allow them to download assignments and communicate with teachers simply by plugging in to a telephone outlet.

On the administrative side, in order to enable teachers to keep track of students' locations as they move from place to place, the Kentucky Migrant Technology Project is developing an Internet based registry that will contain basic information about each student including, last school attended, grades and demographic data. The project has had some success in its initial years and shows great promise in helping educators and migrant students overcome some of the barriers to educational progress. While Internet technology and communication devices cannot exactly reproduce the classroom instructional dynamic, these tools play a critical role in bringing the classroom to a

---

3. Kentucky Migrant Technology Project, *Kentucky Migrant Technology Project/Project Information Summary* (2000).
   4. *Id.*
   5. *Id.*

group of students who, but for this technological innovation, would have limited opportunities for educational advancement.

Web Pages

Creating and posting web pages on the World Wide Web (WWW) represents yet another form of global communication. While utilizing this means of communication is a bit more difficult than setting up an e-mail account, web pages can nevertheless be just as expressive and deliver at least as much content as e-mail communications. Several years ago, when the notion of using the WWW as a means for displaying graphics and transmitting sounds across the Internet was gaining widespread public acceptance, the learning curve to implement this technology tool was relatively steep for the average layperson. For example, those who wanted to create a web page for commercial or personal use typically had to learn Hypertext Markup Language (HTML), a special programming code that enables web pages to be displayed on the WWW. Or, in the alternative, web page hopefuls had to pay someone else to create the page, usually at a significant cost. Prospective web site owners also had to secure space on a network server to display their web pages, much like a prospective home builder would have to purchase a lot on which to build the home.

Over the last couple of years, the process of creating web pages has been simplified to the point that grade school children can become adept at creating and displaying web sites in very little time. Software programs now enable users to point and click and enter text on their web sites without having to know a single bit of HTML. The downside of some of these programs though is that they are geared toward professional or semi-professional web designers and may require hours to master, which can seem daunting to an Internet novice who wants to create a simple family website. In addition to the simplified content creation process, it is now relatively easy to obtain space on a network server to display web sites because most Internet Service Providers allot customers a certain amount of virtual space on their servers to store and display web pages as part of the monthly usage fee. Many ISPs also recognize that the majority of their customers will not be HTML experts nor will they want to devote several hours to learning a software program in order to display a simple web page. Therefore, a number of ISPs now offer web page templates that merely require users to enter information into a preformatted file, which will then be displayed according to the user's preferences.

Each web site on the WWW has its own personal "address" commonly known as a URL (Uniform Resource Locator), which is analogous to a home address. Potential visitors to the site simply type the URL into a web browser and they are immediately taken to the web site associated with that particular address. As the Internet has become more business and e-commerce oriented, URLs or "domain names" have become hot commodities. Catchy or memorable URLs can make an enormous difference in terms of whether potential visitors are able to easily remember and locate web pages and the products associated with them. Thus, merchants with brand name or specialized products to sell online will typically obtain a URL that is closely associated with the product or brand to enable users to easily locate the web site. Or, in some cases, if the web page has a specialized focus, such as increasing black awareness of investment opportunities, then the URL will be descriptive enough so that users can easily locate that content on the WWW (e.g., Blackstocks.com).

Because this communication tool can be uniquely tailored to individual preferences, web sites are often thought of as a personal slice of the Internet landscape where users can express interests, feelings and opinions to the world. And indeed pages on the WWW are literally broadcast to the world because anyone with access to a computer and an Internet connection can view the web site providing they can access the URL. While this form of communicating with Internet technology doesn't provide the intimate feel of one-to-one e-mail correspondence, it does afford a means to communicate personal insights and views to a wider audience. Also, in the new e-commerce economy, web pages provide Internet entrepreneurs with access to global markets for a fraction of the expense that similar "real world" global access to markets might entail. By using the Internet as a means to market their wares, many businesses realize the economies of scale associated with being able to deal directly with consumers. Although using the Internet as a vehicle for e-commerce is explored more in the next chapter, it bears emphasizing here that because Internet merchants are using web pages to communicate, they can either make or break a potential sales transaction with the technology and content used to promote their products. In that regard, first impressions are lasting impressions in the Internet environment and web surfers are notoriously unforgiving of web sites that are poorly designed or complex and confusing to navigate.

While it is fair to say that the WWW has become more business and e-commerce driven in the recent past, there are still a multitude of personal and/or informational web sites that expose web surfers to a host of thoughts, ideas, opinions and cultures. As might be expected in a milieu where practically anything goes, web page content can range from the sublime to the ridiculous. But, notwithstanding this wide-ranging content, one of the complaints frequently leveled against the WWW in its early stages was that it lacked diversity and was therefore of little interest and relevance to minority communities. Recently, however, recognizing the fact that the fastest growing online community is currently black Americans, sites such as Net-Noir.com and BET.com are attempting to respond to that criticism by establishing one-stop portals with relevant and useful content geared primarily toward the black community.

On its web site, NetNoir describes itself as the "leading media destination connecting people and business to Black culture and lifestyle." Further, its goal is to "be the premier location where anyone interested in Black culture, heritage and lifestyle can come for information, products and interaction . . . [and] a portal into the global Black experience." On its home page, NetNoir features several information and activity sections. For instance, visitors can read the latest news, (which has a special focus on black issues), they can visit one of the NetNoir online communities for a chat, or they can visit the gospel chapel for information on the latest gospel music and weekly inspirational messages. If visitors want to find black or African inspired merchandise, NetNoir provides a hypertext link to Blackshopping.com, which offers such specialized merchandise.

BET.com offers similar content "tailored to the needs of African American and urban communities." Not surprisingly, BET.com takes advantage of its tie-in with the Black Entertainment Television (BET) cable network and prominently features content related to online urban music enjoyment. Additionally, recognizing the critical importance of encouraging black Americans to embrace technology, BET.com devotes a special section to technology features. The technology section includes ideas for creating personal web pages, technology product reviews and special news features related to computer technology issues. In June 2000, BET.com announced a partnership with Fannie Mae, Cendant Mortgage and HomeSide Lending to create BET.com Home Center. In furtherance of its goals of educating and empowering black Americans, the Home Center will offer enabling tools and financial applications that allow users to explore mortgage information and apply for home loans online.

In a similar vein, BlackVoices.com, another Internet portal aimed at the black community, recently announced an alliance with automobile giant General Motors (GM) to enable GM to "establish online relationships with the African-American community." According to Barry Cooper, founder and CEO of BlackVoices.com, as part of this strategic Internet alliance, visitors to the BlackVoices web site will be able to explore purchasing a GM vehicle online and interact with GM executives and engineers concerning the vehicles. Additionally, GM will utilize the BlackVoices Career Center to identify and recruit black professionals and suppliers. Clearly such alliances allow specialized focus web sites to offer their constituents expanded access to information and opportunity. In exchange, the corporations forming such partnerships gain access to a captive community of buyers they might not otherwise reach with traditional marketing approaches.

Black stocks and mutual funds are the chief focus of Blackstocks. com, whose motto is "Black America's Place to Create Wealth." The web site describes its mission as getting "African Americans, other minorities and people in general excited about the stock market and investment opportunities." According to the web site, blacks do not participate in the stock market due to a "lack of knowledge, understanding, lack of trust in financial advisors and misperceptions about the market." The site aims to break down those barriers to participation by providing "insightful information, tips, and strategies on how to make money and prosper in the [stock market]." [6]

Finally, IMDiversity.com offers access to the largest database of employers committed to equal opportunity and workplace diversity. The web site reaches out to a number of minority groups and is organized in "villages" that have specialized content for each minority group, such as the African-American Village and the Native American Village. The site's mission is to not only assist job seekers with finding employment, but to provide timely and relevant information to help new employees succeed on the job. The site also endeavors to ensure that visitors achieve personal fulfillment by providing political, economic and spiritual information specific to each ethnic group.

These are but a few examples of the numerous ways in which web pages and the Internet may be used as communication portals to reach out to black Americans in an effort to make the Internet experience relevant to their lifestyles. The enormous potential for these specialized focus web sites to assist in closing the digital divide should not be underestimated. As will be discussed in greater detail in Chapter 8, lack of access to technology is just one factor contributing to the technology gap. The other key factor is relevance, i.e., black Americans don't feel the need for access because of the widespread belief that existing Internet content is not relevant to their experiences. Web sites such as NetNoir.com and BET.com go a long way toward addressing this complaint and removing one of the barriers to closing the digital divide.

Discussion Groups and Chat Rooms

Internet discussion groups and chat rooms provide yet another means for people to communicate across great distances. Unlike e-

---

6. Blackstocks.com, *The Company "Black America's Place to Create Wealth"*, (visited 12/27/00) <http://www.blackstocks.com/abtus/Purpose6.html>.

mail, these communication formats often involve the exchange of information with virtual strangers and are usually at least nominally focused on specific topics. Communicating via discussion groups or chat rooms provides users with the closest approximation of a global networked community. Indeed, friendships have developed across continents and relationships and marriages have been formed as a result of meeting and communicating through these online media. As one author describes it,

> The Internet is not about technology, it is not about information, it is about communication-people talking with each other, people exchanging e-mail, people doing the low ASCII dance. The Internet is mass participation in fully bi-directional, uncensored mass communication. Communication is the basis, the foundation, the radical ground and root upon which all community stands, grows and thrives. The Internet is a community of chronic communicators.[7]

Although the inherent dangers associated with meeting strangers on the Internet should not be minimized, these virtual methods of interacting serve a unique purpose in the lives of many because they allow an instantaneous expansion of one's environment and world view. Moreover, because these communications are typically textual messages scrolling across the computer screen, users can often preserve anonymity and engage in at-will identity shifting. As observers of Internet communication media observe, we are all bodiless in cyberspace, and cannot see race, gender, age or physical appearance. Therefore, these factors do not become relevant unless one chooses to make them so. What this suggests is that these types of virtual communities break down real life boundaries between people whether they be physical or psychological. In fact, some people report feeling a greater sense of freedom and ability to "let their guards down" and express themselves when they aren't being instantly evaluated and categorized as so often happens in face-to-face encoun-

---

7. Michael Strangelove, *The Internet, Electric Gaia and the Rise of the Uncensored Self* 1 5 Computer-Mediated Communication Magazine, 11 (September 1, 1994) (visited 12/27/00) <http://www.december.com/cmc/mag/1994/sep/self.html>.

ters. With the freedom afforded by the anonymous virtual world, there is a greater willingness to try on different online identities because there are usually no repercussions for such behavior, i.e., one can simply discard an identity and don another should one become uncomfortable. As author and computer researcher Sherry Turkle points out, discussion groups and chat rooms on the Internet are "laboratories for the construction of identity."[8] While trying out these identities, real communication takes place as people "exchange pleasantries and argue, engage in intellectual discourse, conduct commerce, exchange knowledge, share emotional support, make plans, brainstorm, gossip, feud, fall in love, find friends and lose them, play games, flirt, create a little high art and a lot of idle talk."[9] Indeed, although author Howard Rheingold initially considered the idea of a virtual community that existed only via a computer screen as "cold," he quickly learned that "people can feel passionately about e-mail and computer conferences."[10] He eventually became one of these people and developed an emotional attachment to the "invisible friends" he met through his computer.

Of course there are those who remain skeptical of this medium's usefulness as a tool for fostering genuine relationships and describe virtual communities as the "illusion of community" where only shallow, impersonal, and often hostile relationships are created. In addition, because online participants receive fewer social context cues and are unable to reduce uncertainty about other participants, naysayers insist that personal relationships cannot be developed or sustained because communication in this environment so often breaks down into posturing and flaming to achieve status within the virtual community.[11] Still others contend that an increasing empha-

---

8. SHERRY TURKLE, LIFE ON THE SCREEN: IDENTITY IN THE AGE OF THE INTERNET 184 (1997).

9. HOWARD RHEINGOLD, THE VIRTUAL COMMUNITY: HOMESTEADING ON THE ELECTRONIC FRONTIER 3 (1993).

10. *Id.* at 1.

11. Brittney G. Chenault, *Developing Personal and Emotional Relationships Via Computer-Mediated Communication* 5 5 Computer-Mediated Communication Magazine, 1 (May, 1998) (visited 12/27/00) <http://www.december.com/cmc/mag/1998/may/chenault.html>.

sis on virtual communities may cause some to "tune out" real-life human interaction and experience increasing levels of personal isolation despite their claims of feeling connected to their "virtual communities."

While these criticisms of virtual community building may be somewhat exaggerated, one thing is certain about online communication: there are real dangers associated with this new medium. In some instances, the openness of online communication can increase the perceived level of trust and lessen the degree of wariness that individuals normally exhibit when meeting strangers. Yet, the feelings of closeness and intimacy transmitted in virtual space may not necessarily be duplicated in real space. In fact, face-to-face encounters often reveal personalities that are markedly different from online personas and can "bring a person into contact with bitter, even dangerous people."[12] Often, this revelation merely leads the individuals concerned to either break off communication altogether or to simply maintain their interaction as an online relationship without any further real-life contact. But, then again, sometimes these encounters can lead to disappointment, fraud, and even death.

For example, in December 1998, Henry A. Ginyard, a sixty-year old cyberspace scam artist, posed as Brett D. Scott and allegedly stole more than $100,000 from eight women he romanced online. Ginyard would apparently search for vulnerable women in Internet chat rooms and tell them a "smooth-sounding hard luck story."[13] After a bit of online contact, Ginyard would tell the women that he was in love with them and even became engaged to several women at a time. Most of the women felt so connected to him that eventually, when he broached the subject of money, they were more than willing to open their purses and credit cards to him. Sadly, some of his victims were forced into bankruptcy when he absconded with their cash and other valuables.

---

12. *Id.*

13. Todd Venezia, *Online Lover Accused of Scamming Women* APB-News.com (December 9, 1998) (visited 12/27/00) <http://www.apbnews.com/newscenter/breakingnews/1998/12/09/online1209_01.html>.

In other online meeting cases, the stakes are much higher than a loss of money, and victims pay with their lives. To illustrate: In January 1999, William Miller killed Joann Marie Brown with a shotgun blast to the head after she refused to end their relationship. According to police reports, Miller met Brown on the Internet and within six months, Brown had moved from her home in Michigan to Missouri to live with Miller. After six months, Miller simply couldn't stand living with Brown anymore and wanted her to leave his home. When she wouldn't, he killed her in cold-blood.[14]

Would the victims in these cases have been more cautious and deliberate in their decision making processes had it not been for the illusion of community and connectedness fostered by the Internet? Although we may never know the answer to this question, these examples illustrate the tragic consequences that can result from the false intimacy created within these virtual communities. One might, however, counter this harsh conclusion with the observation that *every* new encounter contains some degree of risk and simply because online communication may engender a greater *sense* of connectedness, one should not use it as a substitute for the typical familiarization process that takes place when strangers meet. Instead, online communication with strangers might be best viewed as an *additional* cost-efficient way to expand one's horizons and reach out to a global community.

The notion of reaching beyond one's physical boundaries and seeing a world of possibilities is a theme that is frequently echoed in low-income neighborhoods where life choices can appear dramatically restricted because of negative influences in those environments. Although the Internet is certainly no panacea for curing the ills of low-income neighborhoods and schools, it can literally place a wealth of information at one's fingertips. It is a vast library unmatched by any other in the world. Children who aspire to become astronauts but don't have adequate science textbooks in their schools can visit the NASA web site and not only learn about careers in space, but also interact with real-life astronauts. High school stu-

---

14. Todd Venezia, *Online Relationship Ends in Death* APBNews.com (February 2, 1999) (visited 12/27/00).

dents who are interested in college, but don't have access to appropriate mentoring relationships can locate a college web site and establish contact with counselors and alumni who will gladly assist them in their search for a college.[15] Those who are searching for new educational and/or career opportunities can locate an abundance of material by simply entering their specific criteria into an Internet search engine. Senior citizens concerned about health issues can research a growing number of reliable medical web sites and engage in a variety of support group discussions focused on health topics of particular interest to them. In short, the ability to communicate and network on the Internet opens doors that may have been closed by life circumstances, expands opportunities, empowers communities and can make a real difference in the lives of black Americans. Given these circumstances, the question is not whether minority communities should embrace Internet technology, but how soon?

---

15. The use of e-mail to establish mentoring relationships between professionals and middle- and high school students is currently being explored by various mentoring organizations and, in the early stages, has shown some promise for success. The convenience of e-mail as well as the ability to cross numerous practical and interpersonal boundaries has drawn professionals and students alike to these 21st century e-mentoring relationships.

Chapter 5

The E-Commerce Revolution

E-commerce has been variously defined as any transaction that involves an electronic communication on the Internet to the very specific buying and selling activity that now takes place online each day. In this chapter, the discussion of e-commerce will focus almost exclusively on the latter definition. This is because the shift of many everyday activities such as shopping and banking to the Internet has created a vast global marketplace that, in many instances, provides savings and convenience to participants. Of course, those who don't have access are foreclosed from these opportunities to simplify their lives and, perhaps more importantly, save resources.[1]

The E-Commerce Revolution

The Internet has indeed come a long way from its early days when it served primarily as a convenient means for communication among the military and academics. During the 1990s, entrepreneurs realized that the Internet offered enormous potential for virtually unlimited access to global markets. This realization eventually

---

1. In her article, *A Small Town Reveals America's Digital Divide*, Stepanek describes how those connected to the low cost BEV Internet access program were able to save money by comparison price shopping online for services. For example, one member saved $500 on washing machine repairs and $600 on rental trucks.

spawned a "dot.com" revolution as retailers and content providers raced to take advantage of the "e-customer" phenomenon. In a recent report, the United States Commerce department predicted that the digital economy could reach $300 billion by 2002. The report further described how, at the end of 1997, the digital economy grew at double the rate of the general economy and information technology was responsible for more than a quarter of real economic growth in the United States.

On a broad scale, this e-commerce revolution indicates that technology is changing the way individuals and corporations do business. It is also bringing goods and services closer to relevant markets, often eliminating the costs associated with middlemen. But, exactly what are the goods and services that comprise this global electronic business transformation? And what benefits accrue to those participating in this digital economy? And finally, why is it so important that no one be left behind in this new economy? The answers to these questions are often lost amidst the hype surrounding the "dot.com" rage. Although many predicted that the Internet would change every aspect of our daily lives practically overnight, those dramatic predictions have been scaled back and most now believe that the real impact of the Internet remains to be seen. To date, however, the Internet has made significant inroads in several key areas that make it relevant and useful to everyday life experiences. More specifically, the Internet has given users unprecedented purchasing power and informational resources. This technology has also made it easier than ever to pursue educational and employment objectives. This chapter will examine in closer detail some of the tangible and intangible benefits that accrue to those who are able to take advantage of the digital revolution.

Purchasing Power and Convenience

Buying and selling merchandise on the Internet is a primary component of what is currently defined as e-commerce. Each day, millions of people enter the online environment to purchase retail items such as computers, cars, books, airline tickets and clothes. When asked why they shop online, many cite the convenience of shopping at any hour and the potential savings associated with obtaining comparison pricing information. Although there are some lingering concerns about data privacy and security, innovations in secure online shopping and privacy policies have helped consumers overcome those fears and jump headlong into the e-commerce arena. Indeed, during the most recent peak Christmas holiday buying week, online sales surpassed $200 billion in a single day for the first time ever. Outside the holiday seasons, online sales continue a gradual upward trend. For example, in the first quarter of the year 2000, the U.S. Department of Commerce reported that e-commerce sales rose 1.2 percent to $5.26 billion, despite an 8.9 percent decline in overall retail sales. According to Commerce Undersecretary Robert Shapiro, the fact that e-commerce grew at all during the normal post-holiday shopping decline is a sign of its further strengthening and acceptance as a routine way of shopping. A later Commerce Department report for the third quarter of the year 2000 revealed that online retail sales had reached nearly $6.4 billion, a 15.3 percent increase from the previous quarter and the largest percentage increase since the Commerce Department began tracking e-commerce sales figures. While there is some uncertainty as to whether the increase represents more people shopping online or the same customers developing a comfort level with purchasing big ticket items, the upward trend is nevertheless promising.

The Making of a Dot.com Empire

The "dot.com" revolution is so named because Internet retailers typically adopt domain names that are followed by a period ("dot") and the word "com," which is short for commercial and symbolizes the profit-oriented nature of web sites with this suffix. For example, one of the Internet's major e-tailers, Amazon.com, began as an online bookseller and has gradually expanded its operations to include music, electronics, software, toys and collectibles. However, in addition to the retail aspect of Amazon, visitors to the site will also discover a learning experience. For instance, users can read book excerpts and music reviews and occasionally interact with best-selling authors and musicians. With its diversified selling approach, many believe that Amazon has staying power in the sometimes unpredictable e-commerce arena and is, in fact, the prototypical online sales model to which every e-business should aspire. Moreover, many contend that even though Amazon has yet to show a profit, it will nevertheless be a major player in the e-commerce industry for years to come. In a recent article entitled, *"Why Amazon.com Will Survive in the Net Jungle,"* Mike Ogden proclaimed that Amazon will survive simply because "Amazon does it right."[2] Ogden identifies several fundamental reasons why Amazon will achieve long-term stability. First, Amazon's e-commerce processing technology and fulfillment systems are unparalleled in the industry. Indeed, other major retailers such as Toys 'R' Us and Wal-Mart have partnered with Amazon to take advantage of its systems. Second, Amazon provides more value for its customers' dollars. Ogden uses the example of a customer shopping for a DVD player at Amazon.com vs. Walmart.com. While customers will get discounts on the merchandise at both web sites, the Amazon shopper will get editorial reviews, customer ratings/reviews and a buyer's guide for home theater. This constitutes a total shopping experience that makes Amazon's customers more knowledgeable shoppers and breeds loyalty among its vast customer base. Finally, Amazon has adopted a unique approach to customer service that relies entirely on e-mail contact with customers and touts a liberal return policy, both of which have helped earn it a 60% repeat customer rate. Essentially, Amazon reins as top e-tailer because it has identified products that people want and are willing to buy online and it delivers those products conveniently and efficiently.

Another major Internet e-commerce site has almost an identical level of name recognition as Amazon, but has not fared nearly as well in the customer service department. Priceline.com, a popular site for those with savings in mind, offers a unique type of Internet

---

2. Mike Ogden, *Why Amazon Will Survive in the Net Jungle* Austin Business Journal (December 25, 2000) (visited 12/28/00) <http://www.bizjournals.com/austin/stories/2000/12/25/smallb2.html>.

shopping experience that isn't easily duplicated in the non-virtual world.[3] Priceline's distinctive marketing premise is that customers "name their own prices" for goods and services and are therefore able to afford opportunities that might otherwise fall beyond their financial grasp. On the website, customers can set their own prices on goods and services such as airline tickets, hotel rooms, cars, mortgages, groceries and long distance services. Priceline's business model represents a novel approach to saving money on luxury items and necessities in the e-commerce world and, at its inception, was heralded as the shopping experience of the future. After all, isn't it the ultimate consumer "power play" to name the price you're willing to pay for merchandise?

Priceline refers to its brand of e-commerce as a "demand collection system" whereby consumers save money and sellers generate incremental revenue. As a trade-off for these savings, however, consumers are required to be flexible in their brand choices and must leave their offers open for a certain period of time to allow sellers to consider and accept the offers. For instance, when bidding on airline tickets, customers are sometimes told that in order to get their target price, they must travel at certain times and with certain airlines. In the beginning, customers were apparently willing to tolerate a little inconvenience to save money on airline travel. But, over time, several problems developed in Priceline's system, leading one state's Better Business Bureau to blacklist the company. Among the troubles that plagued Priceline were confusing web site terminology that resulted in consumers being unable to tell when they were purchasing products as opposed to getting quotes, surprising additional charges on airline ticket purchases that were not made known to the consumer at the time of purchase and an inadequate customer service staff to respond to customer complaints. The general consensus it seems is that Priceline failed to back up a great idea with great customer service.

In light of its recent troubles, Priceline is reorganizing its business and pledging to refocus its efforts on customer service. Although

---

3. Priceline is also well known for its clever use of pitchman William Shatner, who, in a parody of his own short-lived singing career, sings the graces of Priceline in television commercials.

this is a welcome resolution to Priceline's problems, it may have come a bit too late as major airlines such as United and Northwest have partnered with Hotwire.com to provide competition to Priceline's airline ticket business. If there is one lesson to be learned from the Amazon and Priceline experiences, it is that even though e-commerce represents a new way of conducting business, the old sales cliché, which teaches that the "customer comes first," still applies. In fact, this may be even more applicable in the e-commerce environment where businesses are likely to attract customers who are new to the Internet and skittish about conducting virtual transactions. To lure and maintain these customers, online businesses must convince consumers that there is indeed a "live person" safety net should there be problems with the virtual transaction. In other words, if "[y]ou're stranded in an airport a thousand miles from home [and] your luggage is 33,000 feet above the ground, on a plane headed for who knows where, and you've missed your non-transferable connection for some reason, [then] customer service...needs to be not just adequate, not just good, but incredible."[4]

Internet auction sites represent another type of online shopping experience that allows customers to name their own prices. In fact, auction web sites have become so popular over the last several years that research studies now estimate that online auction sales will total about $25 billion by 2005. eBay.com, which is the largest and perhaps most popular of the many auction sites, offers consumers an opportunity to purchase new and used items from merchants and individual sellers. Just as in the non-virtual world, Internet auctions require consumers to bid against other consumers for merchandise during a set period of time. At the eBay web site, customers can bid on anything from authentic Civil War memorabilia to a two-bedroom townhouse. Clearly, the auction form of e-commerce selling epitomizes the saying "one man's garbage is another man's treasure" and arguably creates the world's largest neighborhood garage sale. Of course, unlike real world garage sales or auctions, bidders are unable to touch and examine the merchandise prior to bidding, which

---

4. Keith Regan, *The Name-Your-Problem E-Tailer* E-Commerce Times (December 11, 2000) (visited 12/28/00).

means that Internet auctions have some disadvantages that are unique to this medium.

For example, in the Internet auction setting, bidders are typically dealing with private sellers, which means that there is no guarantee that the products being offered will be delivered as promised. Unfortunately, the criminal element has also infiltrated the virtual world and many prospective purchasers have lost money at auction sites bidding on non-existent or inauthentic items. As one U.S. Attorney describes Internet auction fraud, "[i]t's an old-fashioned fraud using new technology: promising products and not delivering...[b]ut using the Internet gives the defendants the ability to reach victims all across the country."[5] In a recently uncovered eBay fraud, federal authorities arrested a man who was allegedly offering computers and other merchandise for auction and failing to deliver the merchandise. He is believed to have bilked over 240 victims out of more than $110,000. To be certain, eBay is not the only Internet auction site to be targeted as a medium for unscrupulous criminal behavior and, indeed, eBay representatives have taken appropriate steps to ensure that fraud is a rarity on the web site. Among the safeguards offered by eBay are escrow accounts, which allow buyers to hold payments until goods are delivered. eBay also offers consumers the option of obtaining up to $200 in free insurance.

Another disadvantage of online auctions is related to the bidding process. In real-life auctions, bidders can at least see the other individuals who are bidding on the same item. In the virtual world, however, one must trust that there are really other disinterested parties bidding on the items as opposed to the owner of the property or his confederates bidding under false online identities in order to increase the price of the merchandise, a practice known as "shill bidding." In an attempt to prevent this type of fraudulent activity from occurring, eBay developed the first online shill bidding detection tool in 1999, as a way of analyzing bidding patterns over completed multiple listings. eBay and other auction sites also warn that "shill bidding" could fall under the federal wire fraud statute and violators

---

5. CNNfn.com, *Fraud on E-Bay Alleged* (visited 12/28/00) <http://cnnfn.com/2000/12/27/technology/wires/ebay_wg/>.

could face stiff penalties if caught engaging in this practice. Despite the disadvantages unique to the virtual environment, online auction sites have emerged as a quick and easy way for people to conduct "online garage sales" and for buyers to locate hard to find items at reasonable prices.

The Internet also provides a convenient mechanism for consumers to research and ultimately purchase large ticket items. Web sites such as CarPoint and Autobytel provide a wealth of information on buying and selling new and used vehicles. In addition, these sites offer car buying services, which allow consumers to select and purchase vehicles entirely on the Internet. Because all of the negotiations take place on the Internet, the "haggling" process that has been shown to disadvantage some categories of buyers (namely, minorities and women), is removed from the transaction, allowing for a smoother and potentially less biased purchasing process. Similarly, shopping for a home in just about any price range is as easy as clicking the computer mouse. Web sites such as Realtor.com furnish home buyers and sellers with a wealth of resources, including direct contact with mortgage lenders who can provide rapid responses to online mortgage applications. Again, this virtual process may be especially helpful to minority group members who routinely encounter bias in obtaining home loans.

Even for shoppers who don't want to complete big-ticket purchases online, the Internet is an excellent resource for competitive pricing research. That is, consumers can easily locate relevant information about a desired item and by doing so gain significant bargaining power in the subsequent face-to-face transaction. This is particularly true in the auto sales area, where few transactions are completed online, but consumers are able to bargain much harder at dealerships because they are armed with price information.[6]

One other practical financial advantage that arises from shopping online is that, at least for the time being, many purchases are not subject to sales tax. This is because, under current law, retailers do

---

6. In an interesting twist, aggressive car salespeople, determined not to be outdone by knowledgeable consumers, have been known to declare that information on the Internet is either untrue or outdated.

not collect sales tax on purchases unless they have a physical presence, e.g., facilities or employees, in the state where the buyer is located.[7] So, for example, if an online purchaser lives in Arizona and the online seller has its offices and warehouses in Washington state and has no physical presence in Arizona, then the retailer does not have to collect sales tax from the Arizona purchaser. The physical presence requirement was instituted before the advent of Internet sales and was based upon the belief that disparities in sales tax rules among the states would create logistical nightmares and burdensome compliance costs for mail-order companies. In turn, this would negatively affect interstate commerce. However, with the growth of e-commerce, state and local governments are facing two immediate concerns that were not present with mail-order catalogs. First, the erosion of the state's sales tax base as more and more people are attracted to shopping online. The concern here is that shrinking revenues will impede the state's ability to provide critical governmental services for its citizens. Second, because online sellers are not obligated to collect sales taxes, they are arguably given an unfair advantage over brick and mortar establishments, which will ultimately lose business to the online retail environment.[8]

In response, many state and local governments and brick and mortar retailers are working to simplify the structure of the sales tax collection system recognizing that they stand to lose billions in tax revenue and profits as online sales skyrocket. This simplification process, if agreed upon and passed by the legislatures of the various states, would effectively remove the primary argument that online companies and mail-order catalogs have advanced in favor of foregoing sales tax collection. While all of the legal wrangling is being worked out though, online shoppers can take advantage of yet another cost saving feature of the digital economy.

---

7. Technically, consumers are required to voluntarily remit a use tax to the state for maintenance and use of property in the state. However, consumers rarely fulfill this obligation and there is no current enforcement mechanism to compel substantial compliance.

8. Of course, the counterargument is that the lack of burdensome sales tax collection requirements is necessary to support the continued growth of the online economy.

The Informational Advantage

In addition to buying and selling products and services, the Internet also provides access to news and information that might otherwise require expensive subscriptions or a trip to the library or local bookstore. At minimum, much of this information can be used as an initial reference point to research myriad issues that arise in everyday life. For example, many people hesitate to seek legal and medical advice until problems reach a crisis point because of the cost associated with obtaining this specialized information and/or a mistrust of legal and medical professionals. In the digital age, web sites sponsored by the American Medical Association and American Bar Association are launching points for locating comprehensive medical and legal information. Of course, because anyone can place information on the Internet, users are routinely cautioned to view such information with appropriate skepticism. Nonetheless, these resources can provide basic information and possibly help some to overcome their initial reluctance to address important personal issues with a professional. Indeed, it appears that in the health care context, Americans have strongly embraced the opportunity to seek such information on the Internet.

A recent poll discovered that the number of Americans looking to the Internet for health care information has doubled to 98 million since 1998.[9] To meet this demand, doctors, hospital and pharmacies currently operate thousands of health web sites and the Internet has become "like a giant, worldwide phone directory...[where] with a little perseverance, a Web denizen can click to find a doctor, refill a prescription, diagnose an illness, research the latest treatments and evaluate a health insurance plan."[10] This free flow of information has the net effect of empowering patients and equalizing the doctor/pa-

---

9. Tim McDonald, *Study: Americans Turning to Net for Health Info* E-Commerce Times (August 10, 2000) (visited 12/28/00).

10. Merck, *The Internet and Your Health: Why the Internet?* (visited 7/1/00) <http://www.nytimes.com/partners/microsites/internethealth/index. health>.

tient relationship. Many health oriented web sites also offer "value added" features including the ability to participate in chat room support groups to discuss issues related to specific illnesses.[11] In striking contrast to the medical community's rapid adoption of Internet technology, individual physicians have been somewhat slow to adapt to the Internet as means for communicating with their patients. Explaining their reluctance, many cite concerns about the ability to maintain confidentiality of patient records due to computer hacking or accidental transmission of information.[12] This concern is particularly acute in the mental health area where people may still suffer discriminatory treatment based upon past mental conditions or addictions.

Hospitals are also gradually jumping onto the e-commerce bandwagon by establishing web sites where patients can "download results of their own x-rays or medical tests, send their doctors questions via e-mail over secured links and even make appointments."[13] In addition to confidentiality issues, this unprecedented access to medical information also raises concerns that patients could misinterpret information if they don't have the benefit of a physician's assistance or commentary at the time they receive the information. One concern that rises above the rest, however, is the pressing need to make consumers aware that some of the health web sites, particularly online pharmacies, are unscrupulous and may even provide illegal prescriptions to the detriment of unwitting purchasers. Accordingly, the best advice for web surfers seeking health information is "caveat emptor."

Television, newspapers and magazines have also taken advantage of the digital revolution. Websites such as CNN, the Wall Street Jour-

---

11. *Id.*

12. Indeed these fears may not be entirely misplaced in light of recently disclosed breaches of medical privacy. For instance, in August 2000, Kaiser Permanente mistakenly sent personal information such as advice on sexually transmitted diseases to the wrong e-mail addresses. J.C. Conklin, *Doctors Balk at Electronic Bills, Records* NewsFactor Network (December 27, 2000) (visited 12/28/00).

13. McDonald, *Looking to Net for Health Info.*

nal, Time Magazine and the New York Times offer access to timely and informative online articles 24 hours a day. Although some of these sites charge a fee for accessing their online content, many are free of charge, including the local newspapers of most of the major cities in the U.S. and many international publications. This type of informational content can help bridge the gap between various communities and create a truly global informational village.

Finance and stock market sites have distinguished themselves as one of the more thriving components of the e-commerce revolution. While investing in the stock market may seem confusing and complicated to the average person, the Internet facilitates the stock transaction process by providing information and step-by-step descriptions regarding investment strategies. For example, web sites such as E*Trade and Ameritrade provide easy on-ramps to the stock market and the potential for wealth accumulation. The sites feature numerous articles and tips aimed at the novice investor. In most instances, for a small initial investment, potential investors can make their first market transaction within a couple of hours of visiting the sites.

Banking online is yet another convenient high-tech innovation. Experts predict that by the year 2004, nearly 23 million Americans will be managing their bank accounts online.[14] As the online banking demand increases, "banks will need to stop thinking about the Internet as an alternative channel and instead think of it as a mainstream channel every bit as important as branches, call centers, and ATMs."[15] Currently, however, online banking adoption rates remain low in comparison to customer bases. But, many predict that as consumers develop more confidence that transactions will be handled securely and accurately, the user base will increase significantly.

Additionally, online banks must develop methods to replicate the real world banking experience in order to encourage maximum adoption of this technology. Typically, when consumers want to conduct business with their banking institutions, they require immedi-

---

14. eBusiness Advisor, *Interest Accruing in Online Banking, According to IDC* eBusiness Advisor (July 20, 2000) (visited 12/28/00) <http://www.id-cresearch.com/eBusiness/press/EBIZ071900pr_c.stm>.

15. *Id.*

ate access. Needless to say, Internet access is not always immediate and technology glitches may occasionally interfere with the need to conduct prompt transactions. Thus, reliable access to technology is critical to the expansion of online banking.

General access to technology by larger, more diverse segments of the population is also required for online banking success. Because a typical bank's consumer base is composed of diverse population groups, the viability of any online service also depends upon securing the participation of this diverse consumer group. To the extent that certain population groups continue to lag behind in the technology arena, the success of online banking will be similarly hampered. Perhaps this common sense calculus is what motivated Fleet Bank to invest in a program designed to narrow the digital divide.

The Educational Advantage

Before the Internet, those wishing to advance their education or careers while still maintaining "day" jobs had but a few options. They could either take classes at the local university or register for correspondence courses via the mail. Of course, taking classes at the local college or university often involves a commute after work or on weekends and several hours of in-class time. For anyone who has put in an 8–10 hour day at work, sitting in a classroom and paying careful attention can be the ultimate challenge. Additionally, taking classes usually requires juggling schedules to accommodate courses when they are offered. In contrast, taking correspondence courses allows flexibility in scheduling and study arrangements, but frequently correspondence schools lack accreditation and the programs offered are of questionable academic rigor. In short, there are potentially more obstacles to getting additional education than incentives.

The advent of distance education on the Internet is perhaps one of the most important components of the digital revolution. Universities and commercial enterprises have duly embraced the online education model and it is anticipated that online distance learning will generate $1.1 billion in tuition revenue by the year 2002. Making education available to the largest number of people with the widest variety of options has the greatest potential to bridge societal gaps and level the educational playing field. Online courses or "e-learning" offers the convenience of being able to take classes virtually anytime and anywhere as long as computer resources are available. Many of the courses also possess the necessary academic rigor that one would find at the local university because, in many instances, the local university or some other accredited institution is providing the online content.

Online distance learning comes in several different flavors including for credit and non-credit courses, degree and non-degree programs, and technology versus non-technology courses. Many well known and even lesser well known universities and colleges are riding the technological wave and now offer course content over the Internet. For example, two heavyweights in the education arena, Harvard Business School and Stanford's Graduate School of Business recently announced a partnership to jointly develop and deliver online courses. Through this partnership arrangement, the two schools will provide articles, course materials and the ability to interact online with business leaders.

In some cases, schools offer complete degree programs entirely over the Internet. For instance, Western Governors University (WGU), a unique cooperative between several states and schools, offers programs and classes in a number of subject matter areas. WGU caters to a wide range of non-traditional students, including those who are seeking to enhance their education in order to increase employment prospects and those who are simply interested in exploring subject matter areas for their own personal pleasure. Although these programs are tuition based, a number of web sites sponsor free classes for those interested in merely expanding their knowledge in specific areas, such as computers, writing and antique collecting.

In addition to the online offerings from academic institutions, thousands of commercial enterprises are also entering the online education arena with an emphasis on content geared toward technology or business professionals. Many corporations are recognizing the need to continually update the skills of their employees and are taking advantage of these online educational opportunities to efficiently train employees.

To access most of the course content on the Internet, students typically need only a computer, a modem and an Internet Service Provider. Most of the free courses can be accessed by simply going to the web site of the school or company offering the content and submitting a registration form. For those courses that require tuition, payment is generally arranged before accessing the course content. After payment, the materials can be retrieved via a user/password system. Some courses provide all of the necessary content directly on the Internet while others require students to purchase textbooks to supplement the online information. Additionally, some courses establish regular times when the course meets online for "real-time" discussion, while others use a bulletin board system whereby students can post questions or comments that are logged for later viewing by others in the class.

In sum, the variety and scope of online course offerings makes the Internet the medium of choice for those who want to obtain more education while maximizing convenience. Nevertheless, some believe that even though online education has shown great promise in its early stages of development and implementation, more support is necessary both financially and technologically for this form of distance learning to reach its full potential. In fact, in a recent report to the President and Congress of the United States, the Web-Based Education Commission declared that

> the question is no longer if the Internet can be used to transform learning in new and powerful ways... [because] the Commission has found that it can. Nor is the question should we invest the time, the energy and the money necessary to fulfill its promise in defining and shaping new learning opportunity... [because] the Commission believes we should.[16]

The Commission's report calls upon the nation to mobilize in a united effort to realize the full potential of the Internet as an avenue for educational enhancement. In its report, the Commission outlined seven specific goals that, if realized, would make the dream of

---

16. WEB-BASED EDUCATION COMMISSION, THE POWER OF THE INTERNET FOR LEARNING: MOVING FROM PROMISE TO PRACTICE (2000).

equal access to education a reality. Notably, several of these goals are directly aimed at reducing technological inequalities that currently serve as barriers to equal access. For example, the Commission recommends making powerful new Internet resources, especially broadband access, widely and equitably available and affordable for all learners, developing partnerships between the public and private sector to design high quality online educational content that is relevant to diverse communities, and coordinating state policies to develop common and appropriate programs to reach underrepresented populations.[17] The Commission appropriately concludes that we all have a role to play in harnessing the educational potential of this new technology and collectively moving the "power of the Internet for learning from promise to practice."

The Employment Advantage

Securing and maintaining stable employment has traditionally been the best route to personal and financial security. Many employers today have recognized the efficiency of using the Internet as a recruiting and hiring tool for high technology jobs as well as other non-technology related careers. Potential employees have similarly adapted to this new medium as a means to research potential employers and maximize exposure of their skills to the greatest number of companies. With the wealth of business information on the Internet, researching a prospective employer is both easy and inexpensive and can be accomplished entirely online. For instance, research on a particular company might logically begin with visiting the company's website. Since many organizations believe they cannot afford to be without some sort of web presence in today's digital economy, chances are most employers can be located online. However, since the majority of corporate web sites serve the dual purposes of informational and public relations resource, it is advisable to view any information published on the company web site with a critical eye. This means that the corporate web site can be useful for getting a

---

17. *Id.*

feel for the company and determining whether that style fits one's skills, goals and working habits.[18] To determine whether there have been any major news stories about a particular company (i.e., the information the company would be embarrassed to reveal on its own web site), Internet search engines are ideal tools. By simply plugging in the name of the company, a whole host of news articles from a variety of sources may be instantly accessed. Finally, for those with an interest in the company's financial outlook, the Internet also provides numerous resources for locating SEC filings, financial overviews, and, in today's market, the all-important cash burn rate, (i.e., how fast the company is spending its money and how long it can survive without additional cash infusions).

For those attempting to move beyond simply researching and into actively applying for positions, the Internet is quickly becoming the preferred method for job seeking and recruitment. Although initially most of the jobs available on the Internet were technology related, over the past several years, that has changed considerably and major companies now use the Internet as a tool to recruit for jobs ranging from top executive positions to temporary summer help. The online job search process can be implemented in a number of ways. The most popular choice for job seekers today is registering and placing a resume with an Internet site that specializes in jobs, such as Monster.com or Hotjobs.com. Online job seekers might also place a resume on a job bulletin board or simply create a personal web site to display their credentials. To get the best exposure, commercial web sites and bulletin boards offer the most return on one's investment because they also provide the opportunity to search databases of employers who are actively recruiting and, in some cases, the web sites will even match potential employees with prospective employers. Most of these employment sites allow users to post their resumes and other relevant information without charge. Employers are then recruited to the site and are usually charged a fee to access the database of resumes.[19]

---

18. Robyn Peterson, *Researching Companies to Ensure Job Security* Internet.com (November 28, 2000) (visited 12/28/00).

19. In another twist to employment searching that is perhaps unique to the Internet format, at least one site has offered the ability to bid for em-

Overall, the introduction of the Internet into the job search has made the entire procedure just a little less cumbersome and intimidating. Gone are the days of pounding the pavement, going door to door or cold-calling looking for job opportunities. Furthermore, because prospective employees simply submit their resumes over the Internet, the job search process may be easier for individuals who traditionally have difficulty knowing where or how to begin the job hunt or those who may not have the resources to conduct expensive resume writing and mailing campaigns.

Will online job searches lower the unemployment rate? Some believe that the ability to search more carefully for jobs and employees will make both recruits and employers a bit more choosy in their selection process, thus potentially increasing the time of the overall search process.[20] The jury is still out however on just how all of this connectivity will impact the job turnover rate. For some employees, "the grass always seems greener on the other side" and they will likely be forever in search of the highest paycheck and the best benefits package. The Internet will undoubtedly make their frequent job searches much easier. On the other hand, a positive aspect of making abundant employment related information available on the Internet is that employees and employers may learn more about each other in the initial stages of the recruitment dance and thus create more ideal matches that will lead to long-term employment stability.

There is no question that the recruitment and placement landscape for employers and employees has changed as a result of the Internet. Those who become familiar with this technological innovation will have a decided advantage in the job market over those who don't. In fact, a recent study determined that unemployed workers were two-thirds as likely to use the Internet to search for employment opportunities instead of browsing traditional help-wanted ads. It seems that the Internet employment market, known as "e-cruiting," is "rapidly changing the way workers search for jobs and em-

---

ployment at a job auction site. Potential employees and employers can negotiate salaries and hours just as in a regular auction setting.

20. Alan B. Krueger, *Internet is Lowering the Cost of Advertising and Searching for Jobs* NewYorkTimes.com (July 19, 2000) (visited 7/20/00).

ployers recruit workers."[21] Unfortunately, but perhaps predictably, a digital divide exists in the Internet job search realm as the statistics also reveal that unemployed black and Hispanic workers are much less likely to take advantage of the job research resources on the Internet.[22] It is important to note, however, that much of this disparity may be attributed to differential access to technology since the study found that when blacks and Hispanics have Internet access from home, 64% and 57% respectively use the Internet to look for work, as compared to 48% of whites. This finding led Kuhn and Skuterud to conclude that "the racial gap in Internet job searchs among the unemployed is explained *entirely* by differences in access. Given access to the technology, there is absolutely no indication...that blacks or Hispanics would be less inclined to use it in their search for a new job. If anything, they are more likely to do so."[23] Thus, it seems that in the area of employment, access is the barrier, not relevance.

---

21. *Id.*
22. PETER KUHN & MIKAL SKUTERUD, INTERNET AND TRADITIONAL JOB SEARCH METHODS, 1994–1999 (2000).
23. *Id.*

Chapter 6

Entrepreneurship and E-Government

Today, the Internet is widely used as a vehicle for entrepreneurial endeavors. Although originally designed as a means for the military and academics to communicate, it did not take long for corporations and individuals to recognize the potential profits associated with the unprecedented access to global markets provided by the Internet. The emerging Internet economy, commonly referred to as electronic commerce or "e-commerce," is predicted by many to reach into the billion dollar range over the next several years. Of course, wherever there are potential customers, there are usually entrepreneurs seeking potential sales and profits. Because the resources on the Internet can be utilized by anyone with a computer, a modem and some knowledge of HTML (or the funds to pay someone with such knowledge), the Internet has evolved into a fertile landscape for the millions of companies and people who have products and services to sell.

Not content to leave this tremendous communication and sales tool entirely to the private sector, the public sector, i.e., local, state and federal governments, has also jumped on the Internet and e-commerce bandwagon. Gradually, governments are streamlining their processes and paperwork by making some basic functions available to constituents on the Internet. For instance, instead of standing in long lines to take care of mundane activities such as license renewal, citizens in some jurisdictions are or will soon be able to enjoy the convenience of online renewal.

This chapter will focus on how private sector entrepreneurs are taking advantage of Internet technology to generate income and "be their own bosses." It will further explore how the public sector has similarly embraced this burgeoning technology to cut costs, which ultimately results in savings and convenience for taxpayers.

Internet Entrepreneurs: "There's Gold in Them There Bytes!"

Like the gold rush pioneers of the 1800s, entrepreneurs are flocking to the Internet and its promise of opportunity and economic enrichment. Businesses are launching web sites on the Internet everyday, selling everything from soup to nuts, hoping to attract customers to their wares and this modern method of purchasing merchandise. Some of these businesses are entirely online creations, which means they did not exist prior to the Internet, while others are simply "brick and mortar" companies trying to establish an online presence. Additionally, some businesses market and sell products directly to customers, the so-called "B 2 C" companies, while others focus their marketing efforts on other businesses, "the B 2 B" e-commerce model. This unparalleled business expansion has been dubbed the "new economy" and observers note that this period of growth and innovation has created jobs, boosted productivity and driven the economy forward. Although the entire economy is evolving, perhaps the most noticeable changes have occurred in the small business area. Because anyone with a computer can start an online business, small scale entrepreneurs have been eager to take advantage of the low overhead, reduced infrastructure and communication efficiencies afforded by this global network. To be sure, this new Internet-driven economy, with its low cost of entry and doing business, has spelled the end for some real world stores that simply can't compete with their online counterparts. In fact, as a result of this new, aggressive online competition, many real world establishments have either been forced out of business or compelled to refocus their marketing efforts to the online environment simply to remain competitive.

Marketing and selling on the Internet is not a recipe for instant success however. Thus, while the Internet and e-commerce have been a boon to those with entrepreneurial vision, they have also been a bust for many would-be Internet start-up companies. Indeed, the failure of so-called "dot.com" businesses has itself become a marketable Internet idea. Web sites such as Upside.com, Dotcomfailures.com, and Startupfailures.com exist solely to "pay homage to the spate of recently departed Internet companies." A recent visit to the Upside.com web site revealed memorials to several recently defunct dot.coms including Urbandesign.com, a B2B furniture dealer that died November 22, 2000 "despite...efforts to aggressively attract venture funding...." Another casualty, TheMan.com, a male lifestyle web site, signed off after burning through approximately $17 million in capital funding in a twelve month period. Out of an apparent concern for the future employment opportunities of its employees, TheMan.com posted a message on its web site that encouraged people to "check out the resumes of some of [the] company's talented employees." Finally, as testament to the enormous amount of money involved in this new dot.com economy, WebHouse Club, a name-your-price e-commerce site, ran through $300 million in financing in about ten months and left visitors to the site with the simple message: "It's like having your baseball game rained out when you are ahead."

Explanations for the dot.com "shakeout" vary from identifying it as a normal process of any capital-driven society to concluding that a particular business model or idea is simply not sustainable in the Internet environment. In truth, the answer is very likely a combination of both in that one is realistically a function of the other. Nonetheless, the most common reason generally offered for failing in the new economy is cash shortfall and a lack of additional funding sources. Not surprisingly then, the two most important prerequisites for a successful e-commerce business are a sustainable business model and funding. Without these two features, a web-based business simply can't survive the harsh competition for e-commerce dollars. What kinds of ideas are viable as web businesses and where do entrepreneurs obtain money to turn ideas into e-commerce realities? The next couple of sections will address these vital Internet e-commerce issues.

In the Beginning. . . .

The first question a would-be Internet entrepreneur should ask is: "Do I have an idea that is workable in a web-based environment?" What this means is that there are key differences between selling in the real world and marketing in the online environment that determine whether an idea is viable. For example, in the real world, if a customer goes to the mall to purchase a sweater, the customer can clearly see the color, feel the material, and try the sweater on. In the online environment, these tactile experiences, which often go a long way toward closing the sale, are simply not possible. Therefore, to be successful selling this type of merchandise, a web-based business must make an effort to provide customers with online buying experiences that closely approximate the sensory experiences they are likely to have when shopping in the real world. This means that photographs of merchandise must be as clear and detailed as possible and the product descriptions must use key words that trigger familiar imagery in the minds of consumers. In lieu of actually trying the merchandise on, there should be easily identifiable sizing charts available online.[1] Above all, of course, web businesses should at least have liberal return policies so that customers do not have to feel stuck with items before they have had an opportunity to experience them in the real world.

In general, most customers have a price point beyond which they will resist making a purchase without actually seeing and touching the merchandise. For example, the now defunct web site Furniture.com discovered to its dismay that while customers might buy a $10 book online or even an $800 computer, it's quite a different matter to purchase a $2000 couch without being able to sit on it first. But, even without regard to price, there are some items that customers

---

1. Of late, online companies selling clothing items have begun offering customers the choice of constructing a "virtual model" to try on the clothing in order to give the customer an idea of how the merchandise will look on his/her body. When creating the virtual model, customers enter their own body size dimensions so the model can provide the most accurate picture of how the clothing will fit.

can acquire just as conveniently in the real world, which engenders a reluctance to purchase these items online and incur additional shipping costs and possibly sales tax. A prime example of this is pet food and accessories. At least two high profile online pet stores have failed because customers were unwilling to pay significant shipping and handling charges for pet products that they could just as easily obtain from their local retail outlet.

In contrast, books, CDs, computer software and hardware have proven to be extremely marketable ventures on the Internet. The primary reason for this success is that consumers can adequately experience these goods online by reading excerpts, listening to clips and downloading demo software. Additionally, these categories of merchandise are subject to word-of-mouth purchasing in the sense that people are more apt to buy these items on the recommendation of a friend or relative without having any first hand experience with the items. Although there may be some initial consumer concern in the computer hardware and software market about compatibility, once these concerns are allayed either by compatibility charts on the web site or e-mail correspondence with the online company, people generally have no difficulty purchasing these items on the computer, sight unseen. It appears then that the most important factors in determining whether an online business can succeed are selecting products that can be adequately experienced from the web and ensuring that those products can be delivered economically and conveniently.

The Webvan delivery business model presents an illuminating case study that illustrates the evolution of an arguably questionable Internet e-commerce idea. Quite simply, Webvan's premise is to deliver anything to anybody any day of the week. According to some observers, this idea is one of the most grandiose to come down the information superhighway. To be successful with this plan in the short-term, Webvan has to raise at least $1 billion to build a home delivery network and "become more efficient at warehousing and same-day delivery than any other company in the field...." Webvan must also endeavor to fundamentally change consumer shopping behavior. Because their business model is in many respects based upon the idea that consumers, if given the opportunity, would gladly leave the chore of shopping to someone else, Webvan must, in fact, get consumers to alter their normal shopping routines in favor of relying upon an Internet alternative. At the same time however, in order to make the instant delivery idea appeal to the widest audience, Webvan must aggressively promote itself as catering to the consumer's need for instant gratification and follow through by providing same or next-day delivery of everything from soup to nuts. And that, indeed, is Webvan's plan. To implement this plan, "Webvan plans to build a far-flung hub-and-spoke system in each market it enters. Each system will consist of a highly automated distribution center feeding 10 to 12 substations situated within a 50-mile radius. These megawarehouses will store 50,000 different products... [b]y the time Webvan enters 26 markets, it will have spent $1 billion."[2]

Of course, not all e-commerce entrepreneurial ideas are of this magnitude. In fact, one Webvan competitor, GroceryWorks, hopes that by lowering costs and increasing service, it can break into the same day delivery service but on a much smaller and more efficient scale. Specifically, GroceryWorks' logistical design focuses on less handling of the goods and less automation of the process while utilizing smaller warehouses that are closer to customers.[3]

Another characteristic of the e-commerce phenomenon involves "brick and mortar" stores, which are venturing into the online environment in record numbers to provide customers with an Internet alternative. Although many of these established retailers were at first reluctant to enter the online fray, most have embraced the technology with such zeal that they are now predicted to dominate and outlast many of their pure online competitors. With such success, one might wonder why brick and mortar establishments hesitated to go online. In other words, why wouldn't an established brick and mortar retailer take advantage of the e-commerce trend? There are very likely as many reasons as there are retailers, but many seemed to be-

2. Connie Guglielmo, Webvan Article, *ZDNet: Business & Tech E-Commerce: The Works* (visited 5/12/00).
3. Tom Steinert-Threlkeld, GroceryWorks Article, *ZDNet: Business and Tech E-Commerce: GroceryWorks: The Low-Touch Alternative* (visited 5/12/00).

lieve that e-commerce might actually be a fad and were reluctant to siphon off profits from their real world stores to support a project that had a short shelf-life. Additionally, many worried that even if they established a successful online business, its profitability would come at the expense of their real world stores, which would suffer from decreased customer traffic and sales.

Despite these concerns, many traditional retail businesses ultimately chose to establish an e-commerce presence after weighing the benefits associated with going online. For example, without regard to how long a retailer has been in business, chances are that in today's information technology driven society, many of its customers will demand a way to shop more quickly and conveniently. To avoid alienating this portion of its customer base, retailers *must* seriously consider web based shopping alternatives. Additionally, in some cases, retailers were lured by the fact that online sales would likely result in overall cost savings once the initial expenses associated with launching the online component had been absorbed. Finally, given the myriad ways to use the Internet as a communication tool, many retailers probably envisioned an Internet venture as an opportunity to interact with customers in ways that enhance loyalty to their brick and mortar stores and products.

Surprisingly, some brick and mortar establishments have become so enamored with the e-commerce model that they have chosen to eliminate their real world stores and transform into pure dot.com businesses. For example, Nancy Zebrick, who owned a traditional travel agency, launched a web site to complement her brick and mortar store.[4] According to Ms. Zebrick, "[t]he gross profit margins [per sale] are lower online, but we make it up in volume because we can sell nationally, in fact internationally."[5] In light of the global access to markets on the Internet, Ms. Zebrick eventually closed her brick and mortar store, which is certainly an option for other traditional establishments, albeit a risky one. Indeed, many advise brick and mortar establishments to simply keep the storefront and add a

---

4. Robert McGarvey, Retail to e-Tail, *ZDNet:Small Business:Connecting the E-Com Dots* Entrepreneur Magazine (visited 6/12/00).

5. *Id.*

web site because "[t]here are tremendous advantages to be had by leveraging Net sales with a [brick and mortar store]...you can use the store to promote the Web site...[by] printing your Web address on bags, sales slips and advertising fliers..."[6] This can give brick and mortar stores a significant advantage over "stand-alone" dot.coms, which typically have to spend a great deal of money just to get people to visit their web sites.

One crucial aspect of planning an online business that shouldn't be overlooked in the race to "go digital" is "ensuring that the business idea actually reflects a real customer need."[7] According to Varianini and Vaturi, prospective online entrepreneurs must develop as much fact-based knowledge about consumer needs and behavior as possible because such information is critical to determining when the business may legitimately cut corners without sacrificing customer service. The authors conclude that while rushing an idea to the online market is still a consideration in the digital economy, "[t]he challenge for new e-businesses is to deliver what customers want, and will pay for, as quickly as possible—without getting tripped up by the problems that the need for haste creates."[8]

This new Internet economy, which rewards those with an entrepreneurial spirit, could prove to be a godsend to minority entrepreneurs. As discussed in Chapter 2, there is no dearth of creative business ideas in minority communities. The problem involves turning those ideas into reality when the entrepreneurial path is riddled with barriers, many of which have nothing to do with the feasibility of the idea. The Internet presents, at least initially, the promise of equal access to business opportunity for those who take the time to explore this new medium. As the examples discussed above illustrate, there is no one successful business model in the e-commerce arena. Ultimately then, each individual must make the decision as to whether the e-commerce environment will be the key to business success and

---

6. *Id.*
7. Vittoria Varianini & Diana Vaturi, *Marketing Lessons from E-Failures* 4 The McKinsey Quarterly (2000) (visited 12/21/00).
8. *Id.*

wealth accumulation, keeping in mind that even the best business model will not get off the ground without proper financing.

Not surprisingly, the lack of start-up capital is often the primary barrier to progress for minority entrepreneurs. Most observers of the dot.com phenomenon agree that financing for e-commerce business plans has surpassed all expectations, with even marginal ideas receiving the blessing and the dollars of investors who want desperately to jump on the e-commerce bandwagon. The next section will examine the path to financing Internet ventures, which may open the door to economic opportunity for those who have been previously shut out by life circumstances.

"Show Me the Dot.Com Money"

The key to success for any entrepreneurial endeavor is financing. In the early stages of the digital revolution, venture capital funds were available for practically any e-commerce idea. Venture capitalists threw caution to the wind in the e-commerce gold rush and often failed to genuinely consider whether business plans were viable and whether they could ultimately be profitable in the online environment. To understand how atypical this is, one must first be aware that, because venture capital is a risky business and the investments are essentially unprotected in the event of failure, venture capital firms traditionally set fairly rigorous guidelines concerning the venture proposal size, maturity of the seeking company, and evaluation procedures in order to reduce risks.[9] Additionally, because venture capitalists become owners of the companies they finance, they tend to examine business proposals with extreme care, paying particular attention to how soon the company can increase sales and generate substantial profits.[10] Again, this traditionally cautious behavior was sacrificed in the race to grab a piece of the e-commerce pie and, in some cases, the results were nothing

---

9. LaRue Tone Hosmer, Information on Venture Capital for Small Businesses, *A Venture Capital Primer for Small Business* (visited 11/30/00) <http://www.freewell.com/freereports/business/67.html>.

10. *Id.*

short of disaster as companies "burned through" their financing at astounding rates only to close their doors after the business plan proved to be unsuited to the e-commerce arena. Recently, the failure rate of dot.com businesses has forced venture capital firms to once again rely upon their tried and true formula for successful financing, i.e., assessing the long-term viability and potential profitability of a company as a means for determining investment decisions.

Rather than providing all of the funding up front, most venture capital firms offer financing in various stages to assist companies develop from the initial business idea to an initial public offering. For example, the first financing stage when venture capital firms are likely to be involved is the "seed stage." During this stage, venture capital firms typically make a financial commitment between $1–5 million and the funds are generally used by the business for concept and product development. This stage usually occurs after the company is about a year old, although the e-commerce revolution brought venture capital financing into the process at a much earlier stage.[11] The next stages of funding help the company to expand upon its original idea. During these phases, venture capital firms generally invest between $5–10 million to support efforts to enhance the company's presence in the market place.[12] Finally, the mezzanine stage of funding, which typically occurs pre-IPO, allows the company to focus on further research and development, increased marketing and advertising efforts and perhaps even acquisitions of other companies that have compatible goals. After this stage, venture capital firms fully expect that the company will "go public" by issuing an initial public offering of stock, some of which is issued to the venture capital firm. How much stock gets issued to the venture capital firm depends, in part, upon the amount of financing provided, success and worth of the business and the anticipated return on the investment. However, "[m]ost venture firms...don't want a position of more than thirty to forty percent because they want the owner to have the incentive to keep building the business...[and venture capital firms] really want

---

11. meVC ViewPoint, Description of Venture Funding Stages, *The ABC's of Venture Funding Rounds* (visited 11/30/00).
    12. *Id.*

to leave control in the hands of the company's managers, because it is really investing in that management team in the first place."[13]

Since approximately ninety percent of all proposals for venture capital funds are immediately rejected, how does an entrepreneur place herself in the best position to receive venture capital funding? According to Hosmer's *Venture Capital Primer*, the key word is planning. What this means is that the prospective business owner should have well-prepared financial plans and projections that include cash budgets, pro-forma statements, capital investment analysis and capital source studies. Essentially, the more detailed and prepared the business plan, the greater the likelihood that venture capital funds will be forthcoming.

Another way to finance an e-commerce idea is by using the incubator model. Internet incubators are based on the "theory that the Internet has created a land-grab environment, where the companies that can get to market first have a huge advantage."[14] Therefore, Internet incubators, much like our traditional understanding of the word, assist fledgling e-commerce companies to develop in a controlled and supportive environment. For instance, incubators provide start-up companies with human and physical resources such as office space, administrative support, high-speed Internet access and the latest technology. With these necessary (and often expensive) components of a new company taken care of by the incubator, the e-commerce entrepreneurs are free to focus on developing the business. This model is particularly helpful to those with an innovative e-commerce idea who don't possess the technological know-how to launch and maintain an Internet site.

In exchange for providing a supportive start-up environment, incubators, like venture capital firms, generally take an equity stake in the new company, which can be anywhere from 10 to 45 percent. Because the equity stake may be rather large in some cases, it is wise for potential start-up companies to evaluate incubators much like they would evaluate prospective partners in their business. In other

---

13. Hosmer, *Venture Capital Primer*.
14. Mel Duvall & Connie Guglielmo, *ZDNet: Business & Tech E-Commerce: The First Cracks* (visited 5/12/00).

words, entrepreneurs should carefully consider the level of services provided, the amount of control exercised by the incubator and the price of obtaining similar services on the open market without an equity stake commitment.

Although incubators seem to offer an excellent opportunity for e-commerce entrepreneurs to "test their wings," some industry observers remain skeptical about the incubator model. They contend that while a company may appear to be premised upon a viable idea and have all the earmarks of success, the real test comes when the start-up is removed from the artificial incubator environment and forced to go it alone. Thus, in the final analysis, instead of the coddling provided by e-commerce incubators, success as an e-commerce business may well depend upon a "magical confluence of luck, talent, skill and timing."[15]

Whichever path an Internet entrepreneur chooses, it appears that at least in the initial stages of e-commerce development, venture capital financing and incubator space is readily available to those who demonstrate extensive planning and preparation to enter the new economy. Because financing and support seem to be based largely upon workable ideas rather than the race or ethnic background of the entrepreneurs, the e-commerce arena shows genuine promise for equal economic opportunity, which is the starting point for financial stability and ultimately wealth accumulation. Of course, this is not to suggest that racism is completely removed from the dot.com financing process, for that would be much too optimistic. Instead, it is a recognition that perhaps because of the virtual nature of the Internet, where *viable ideas* are the primary currency, the color of the person posing the idea is less important than whether the idea can succeed.

E-Commerce in the Public Sector: E-Government

Given the ease and efficiency of conducting transactions in a virtual environment, it is perhaps not surprising that governments

---

15. *Id.*

would consider adopting e-commerce platforms in an attempt to make their services more accessible to the citizenry. Unlike the private sector, however, there are many more *disincentives* for e-government to embrace Internet technology. First, incubators and millions of dollars in venture capital financing are not readily available to help government agencies make the e-commerce transition. Second, and perhaps more important, governmental entities may be slower to adopt technological innovations because they simply do not have the same competitive incentive for going online that drives their private sector counterparts. The fact is that most government functions are monopoly based services and many are mandatory.[16]

But, notwithstanding the obvious lack of incentives, local, state and federal government agencies are committed to increasing the amount of government information on the Internet and to offering citizens the opportunity to conduct government transactions online. In fact, in December 1999, President Bill Clinton signed a pair of executive memorandums aimed at increasing the amount of government information online and exploring the possibility of e-voting.[17] According to Vice President Gore, who introduced the initiatives, the goal is to make the government as accessible as Internet commerce has made shopping. The Center for Democracy and Technology (CDT) applauded the federal government's efforts and is conducting research into several areas of e-government. One such CDT study posed the question, "What do citizens say they want [from e-government]?"[18] In a variety of surveys conducted by states and research organizations, respondents were asked to reply to this question by choosing from a list of typical government functions, including renewing a driver's license, voter registration, voting on the Internet, "one-stop" government shopping, filing state taxes and accessing medical information. The survey found that renewing a driver's license was typically the first choice followed closely by voter registra-

16. Matthew Symonds, Difficulties of e-Government Transition, *No Gain Without Pain* The Economist (June 24, 2000) (visited 1/7/00).

17. The two memos were unveiled by Vice President Al Gore and were labeled the "E-Government Directive" and the "E-Society Directive."

18. Meghan E. Cook, CDT Survey, *What Citizens Want From E-Government* (visited 5/12/00).

tion. There was also significant support for the ability to access medical or health care data on the Internet.

A separate survey commissioned by the Council for Excellence in Government found that there was broad support among the public for e-government although there was some difference of opinion as to how swiftly the government should transition services to the online environment.[19] In fact, 65 percent of those surveyed believed that government should proceed slowly in light of the serious concerns about security, privacy and access. Perhaps the most remarkable aspect of this study was the participants' reaction to the idea of e-voting. Most expressed opposition to online voting, with security concerns identified as the probable reason for the overwhelmingly negative response. Apparently survey respondents were concerned that the ability to cast their ballots privately and anonymously might be compromised if the voting process were done electronically. That is, the tracking ability inherent in computer technology would allow their votes to ultimately be traced back to them.

In another e-government research study, when asked about funding for e-government services, most citizens preferred to pay a per transaction fee rather than support such services through tax increases. However, this response may, in fact, be a function of familiarity with the services that e-government can provide. That is, a lack of familiarity with technology generally implies a lack of use, which translates into a reluctance to fund such services through tax dollars. Thus, the more familiar and comfortable citizens become with e-government, the more likely they are to regard it as an important governmental function and the more likely they are to prefer using tax dollars to finance e-government services. Although these surveys uncovered differing views on what types of services the government should provide online, market research efforts such as these are necessary and will ultimately facilitate online government processes that are responsive to customers/citizens needs.[20]

---

19. Brock N. Meeks, *Americans High on E-Government* (visited 5/12/00).

20. As soon as governments determine which services they can conveniently and cost-effectively provide online, they will discover that commercial Internet and software companies are ready and willing to smooth the

When making the e-government transition, it is likely that the determination as to whether specific government services are transferred online will involve an extensive cost/benefit analysis by government agencies. While the costs might differ depending upon the type of content provided and the security measures necessary to engender customer confidence, there are enormous benefits for the public and government associated with placing information and services online.[21] For instance, e-government can provide quicker access to information, public access to *more* information, and the ability to reach more people and improve government responsiveness.[22] However, once implemented, there is no easy method for government to measure whether these benefits are actually accruing to the target audience: its citizens. In the private sector, the effectiveness of an e-commerce initiative is measured by profits or the potential for profits after a period of time. Since government agencies do not have a similar profit yardstick, the question becomes, how do we measure the effectiveness of e-government? Do we examine the savings that accrue to taxpayers by providing information online or do we gauge success by whether citizens are actually utilizing the online information or some combination of the two?

For example, the NASA government web site has reduced costs by completely eliminating printing and mailing for news releases in favor of producing electronic versions on its web site.[23] The web site is also interactive in the sense that it offers visitors the opportunity

---

transition of government services to the online environment. Companies such as Microsoft, Election.com and govWorks aim to get a part of the estimated $455 million to $12.5 billion dollars predicted to be spent over the next five years by local, state and federal governments on the e-government process. For example, Microsoft recently struck a deal with the Pennsylvania state government to build a mega-portal for the state; in the online voting arena, Election.com is touting itself as the "premiere provider of online voting services"; and govWorks is developing software that enables governments to provide such services as paying parking tickets online.

21. Heather Harreld, The Value of e-Government Sites, *Measuring E-GOV Value* Federal Computer Week (visited 5/12/00).

22. *Id.*

23. *Id.*

to converse with astronauts and scientists via a live chat, which makes "people feel like they're participating in space programs, as opposed to [being] spectators."[24] Similarly, the Department of Health and Human Service's Healthfinder site, which provides consumer health information, now averages 500,000 hits per month, five times the number of citizens it was able to reach prior to the launch of its site. And, in a compelling illustration of the power of the Internet, when the Federal Consumer Information Center was deluged with requests for a package of documents related to women's issues, they distributed one million printed packages and referred the rest of the requests to their web site.[25] By using the Internet, the agency was able to save money by not printing additional packages and efficiently satisfied the additional consumer demand for the information. Are these successful examples of e-government? They certainly seem to be in that they are cost-efficient and sensitive to citizen demand for responsive government. Therefore, no matter how the success of e-government is eventually measured, citizens will benefit if e-government continues to bring government services closer in line with the needs and expectations of its citizens.

Yet, despite what appears to be favorable progress in the area of e-government, a separate question remains as to whether and to what extent the e-government *technological transition* will be a success. According to Todd Ramsey, IBM's worldwide head of government services, "[a]bout 85% of all public-sector [information technology] projects are deemed to be failures."[26] Part of the reason for this failure is the government procurement process, which often involves implementing a competitive bidding process before any government purchases are made. This process is usually lengthy and may not always result in an outcome that provides value and quality of service. What this means in practical terms is that before a government agency can take the plunge into e-government, it may have to conduct a lengthy bidding process just to purchase the necessary computer hardware and software, resulting in inevitable delays and

---

24. *Id.*
25. *Id.*
26. Symonds, *No Gain.*

the real possibility that the equipment may be outdated when it is eventually installed.

Another technology transition problem is, of course, bureaucratic inertia. Practically everyone is familiar with the stereotype of the government employee who performs functions in a certain manner simply because "they have always been done that way."[27] This employee is the model of inflexibility and impracticality and is unlikely to initially "appreciate" technological change. Therefore, adopting an e-government platform will almost certainly require training programs for current employees who may be unused to and unwilling to adapt to the new environment. But, perhaps the more frightening reality and potential cause for resistance is that technology implementation will almost certainly result in a variety of efficiencies that could eventually lead to downsizing, diminished responsibilities and an elimination of jobs.

Given these internal challenges to success, the key, as Symonds suggests, is for governments to adopt technology in steps or phases. The first step might involve government agencies and departments merely posting relevant information on the Internet.[28] Many governmental entities have accomplished this step with little difficulty and resistance. Once the agency web site is known to its target market, the next step is to allow for some form of interaction or two-way communication with the agency or department via the web site. This might include the option of sending e-mail to appropriate officials or web-based forms that allow users to input information. When citizens are comfortable using the site in an interactive fashion, then a "formal, quantifiable exchange of value" can take place between government and citizen. This exchange of value might include, for example, paying a fine or renewing a license. The final stage is a "one-stop shopping portal" that allows citizens to communicate with government based upon specific needs rather than agencies. This means that users would be able to access any part of government with a single logon to the portal web site.[29]

---

27. To be fair, this characterization may also be applied in the corporate environment.
28. Symonds, *No Gain.*
29. *Id.*

Implementing these e-commerce steps will be "complex and will require not only vision, but also strong political leadership at the highest level."[30] Public acceptance will also require that government be sensitive to the privacy, security and access concerns that serve as barriers to widespread public use and support of e-government.[31] Moreover, once certain private information has been collected electronically from the public, the government must endeavor to assure citizens that their information will be maintained in a confidential manner. Many citizens, including those in minority communities, already fear the potential for collection and misuse of information by the government. Seminars, employee training programs and public relations efforts aimed at ensuring the public of the integrity of the government's information collection processes may go a long way toward easing concerns about the government acting as "Big Brother" and electronically invading the privacy of its citizens. In essence, e-government will only work if government is accountable, transparent and responsive to its citizenry. These factors are likely to be most appealing to those in minority communities who, for some very legitimate reasons, are often suspicious of government and skeptical of its motives. If people perceive that they have greater control over their interactions with the government and can see how processes operate, then those levels of mistrust and skepticism are likely to be reduced. However, one of the costs of reducing mistrust is ensuring that all citizens have equal *access* to the technology that serves as an onramp to e-government.

The Digital Divide, E-Government and E-Voting

In the historic wrangling following the most recent presidential election, one of the claims repeatedly leveled against Florida election

---

30. *Id.*

31. Many suggest that digital signature technology may go a long way toward allaying fears about security and privacy in the e-government environment just as it has done in the private sector.

officials was that many blacks were not only disenfranchised by the voting system in Florida, but were allegedly subjected to biased treatment by police officers and election officials as they traveled to and entered polling places on election night. Additionally, many votes in minority communities were allegedly not counted because outdated and confusing voting machinery caused some to improperly punch their ballots. The question that immediately comes to mind is whether there are e-government solutions that could have made this process easier and less biased. More specifically, could an e-voting procedure have resulted in more valid ballots cast on behalf of black voters in Florida while simultaneously reducing opportunities to inject bias and personal prejudice into the voting system?

Naturally, there are numerous concerns raised by the specter of e-voting, some of which are related to the potential disenfranchisement of minority communities and many of which are related simply to the ability to provide the necessary security to prevent voter fraud by any citizen. The idea of abandoning polling place voting is certainly not a new one and, in fact, in this past election season, the state of Oregon used an entirely mail-in ballot voting system. Nor is it unheard of to cast ballots online. During the presidential primary season, Democrats in Arizona used an online voting process that resulted in a turnout rate that was six times the usual level for a primary election. Thus, the fundamental technology for e-voting is in place and, with the rapid pace of innovation, it will certainly not be long before technology is capable of providing the necessary security to enable citizens to feel comfortable casting ballots online. However, even if e-voting offers the promise of convenient, private online voting with no external interference, are minority voters facing disenfranchisement on another level simply because they do not have *access* to the relevant technology? Considering the current statistics on the digital divide, there is certainly a very strong argument that e-voting will lock millions of blacks out of the voting process. The unfortunate irony here is that the implementation of an innovative e-voting system, designed to ensure maximum and convenient participation in the democratic process would, in fact, be hampered by the legacy of disparate treatment of minority citizens. Nevertheless, given the recent experiences of black citizens in the Florida election fiasco, the notion that a right as cherished and fundamental as voting can be carried out in the privacy of one's own home via a personal computer should be enough of an incentive to convince even the most die-hard technophobe that *technology is indeed relevant and access is crucial to participating in the democratic process.* Again, there is no question that technology will soon accommodate security concerns related to e-voting. The only question that remains is will the alleged victims of disenfranchisement embrace this modern method to conveniently cast ballots close to home and let their voices be heard unfettered by the biases and prejudices that plague our current system of voting.

PART III

SOLUTIONS TO CLOSE THE GAP

Chapter 7

Legal, Practical and Technological Initiatives

The Internet as "Big Brother"

During a recent survey by the Center for Communication Policy at UCLA, when asked if they fear going online endangers their privacy, two-thirds of U.S. Internet users and three-quarters of non-Internet users expressed such fears. It seems that when considering all of the risks associated with Internet usage, the ability to maintain privacy while online is perceived as the greatest danger by far. This fear not only discourages non-Internet users from taking the leap into technology, but also establishes a significant barrier to the overall growth of e-commerce. That is, if users can't be assured that their private information will be safeguarded, then they are far less likely to engage in the kinds of transactions that require disclosure of personal information, such as purchasing products on the Internet. In fact, the survey discovered that 98% of Internet users who have not purchased merchandise online declined to do so because of concerns regarding the security of credit card information.

Unfortunately, the issue of online personal privacy is likely to resurrect tragic memories and reopen old wounds for many in the black community. As discussed in Chapter 1, the notion of vigilantly protecting one's personal privacy is apt to loom large in the minds of many black Americans in light of the documented history of manipulation and abuse by the government and scientific communities.

Under the guise of "scientific" research studies, these entities have, at various points throughout history, gathered information on black people and concluded, among other things, that they are: 1) intellectually inferior to whites and 2) somehow less than human and not entitled to minimal treatment for the ravages of a deadly disease. Given this historical context, it doesn't require a great leap of imagination to conclude that some people might genuinely fear that computer technology is simply another means to gain access to personal information for the purpose of targeting unpopular groups. Thus, in addition to the general fears expressed by many Americans, black Americans, because of their unique historical perspective, are likely to have heightened levels of suspicion when it comes to even utilizing computer technology, much less disclosing personal information on the Internet. Are fears about computers and the Internet evolving into a virtual "Big Brother" the product of ignorance and unchecked paranoia? Consider these examples:

- Predictive Networks, a technology start-up company in Cambridge, Massachusetts, has developed software that tracks which Internet sites users have visited and compiles "click-stream" data to help Internet advertisers achieve their targeted marketing objectives. Because Internet users rarely click advertising banners presented on web pages,[1] this software is particularly attractive to advertisers who want to get their products in front of consumers who are likely to click on the banners and hopefully take the further step of purchasing the product. Thus, by tracking where a person spends time on the Internet, advertisers can develop a more accurate virtual "profile" of an Internet user and target advertising especially designed to attract that user's attention. Are there privacy concerns with this collection and compilation of data? Predictive Networks' founder, Devin Hosea, assures that the process of tracking a user's Internet travels is done with complete anonymity, i.e., nothing specific to the user such as name, address, and telephone number is collected. Addition-

---

1. In fact, the industry average for users clicking on Internet advertising (also known as the click-through rate) is well below one percent.

ally, all the data that identifies which sites the user has visited is later discarded.

- The FBI is currently capable of using a detection system known as "Carnivore" to scan all incoming and outgoing e-mail at an Internet Service Provider (ISP) in search of messages associated with the target of a criminal probe. To intercept the messages, the FBI plugs into the ISP's network system and reviews all the sender and recipient e-mail addresses and subject lines before deciding whether to access a complete version of a particular e-mail. The FBI's rationale for this extensive monitoring practice is that ISPs have complained that they cannot accurately sort out specific e-mail in response to an FBI warrant, therefore, the FBI must implement a system that reviews everything in search of e-mail relevant to the criminal investigation. The ACLU has argued that this type of wholesale monitoring of e-mail traffic over an ISP network is the virtual equivalent of a wiretap capable of accessing the conversations of all of the phone company's customers. Further, the ACLU scoffs at the notion that citizens should trust the government to filter out irrelevant e-mail and only focus on mail that is potentially associated with criminal activity. Indeed, it was recently revealed that the Carnivore system could reliably capture and archive all unfiltered traffic to the internal hard drive of the computer.

- The Office of National Drug Control Policy used software to track computer users who view anti-drug advertisements on the Internet. The office also arranged with certain search engines to display anti-drug advertisements to users who searched using drug terms such as "pot" or "weed."

With so much personal information traveling across the Internet on a daily basis and with consumers expressing heightened concern about the protection of that information, it is perhaps not surprising that Congress would eagerly embrace this issue and propose legislation designed to protect the privacy of those who use the Internet. While the federal government initially took a hands-off approach to regulation of the Internet in favor of allowing the industry to regulate itself, it has become apparent that the industry doesn't always act with the consumer's best interest in mind, particularly in the area of safeguarding private information. As FTC Chairman Robert Pitofsky observed, currently about forty-one percent of web sites provide visitors with a privacy policy and the choice to opt out of providing personal information or limit its use. As a result, the FTC, once an advocate of industry self-regulation, now believes that further compliance by web sites will require "backstop" legislation to ensure that consumers' privacy is protected online. But why is industry self-regulation so lacking that legislation is necessary? Most believe that the deficiency arises from the fact that while the majority of online companies *recognize* the pressing need to protect online consumers' privacy, only a small percentage of sites are *implementing* the four substantive fair information practice principles: notice/awareness, choice/consent, access/participation and security/integrity. Thus, the FTC and many in Congress are confident that legislation will provide the best incentive to encourage online companies to comply with these basic standards of online privacy protection. Before considering some of the recently proposed legislation, the next section will examine the privacy policies of two online companies and analyze whether these guidelines and other self-regulation efforts are sufficiently protective of consumers' privacy so as to obviate the need for legislation.

Privacy Policies

One of the first indications that privacy policies do not rank very highly on the priority lists of most web sites is the fact that hypertext links directing users to such policies are almost always buried in the small print at the very bottom of the web site, well beyond the content section of the page. Most web site visitors would not be expected to scroll down that far on the page since the content is usually the focal point. Nevertheless, many web sites have embraced the movement toward self-regulation and willingly provide consumers with an opportunity to understand how their private information will be treated online. For example, online giant Amazon.com has a very extensive privacy policy, which users agree to accept simply by virtue of visiting the online site. The policy advises customers that Amazon collects private data from several sources, including information that the customer chooses to reveal and information that is automatically gleaned from the customer's web browser through the use of "cookies."[2] The Amazon privacy policy also notifies customers that Amazon shares their personal information with subsidiaries, agents who perform services for Amazon, and for purposes of fraud protection and credit risk reduction. Beyond those instances, the policy assures customers that they will have the opportunity to opt out of having information shared with third parties. According to Amazon's policy, the security of personal information is protected by special software that encrypts the information as it is transmitted across the Internet.

In comparison, online auction site, uBid.com, has a similar, although more specific, online privacy protection policy. uBid's policy first outlines the types of information collected and identifies third parties, such as vendors, who might gain access to the information as part of the online sales process. Further, uBid advises that while it does not sell, trade or rent consumers' personal information, it may provide data about its customers on an aggregated basis to third parties. uBid explains, however, that this aggregated data does not contain any identifiers that would specifically connect the information to particular individuals. uBid also uses special encryption software to protect private information as it travels across the Internet. The privacy policy explains how the encryption software operates and advises customers of corrective action that may be necessary if their browsers do not support the special security features.

What is most interesting about these policies is that they seem to focus primarily on protecting consumer information in the transmission process as the consumer is making an online purchase. Of course this is a laudable objective and one that is certainly welcomed

---

2. Cookies are defined in Amazon's policy as alphanumeric identifiers that are transferred to the user's computer hard drive to enable the Amazon system to recognize the user's browser during each successive visit to the site. By recognizing a user's browser, Amazon can provide the user with a personalized experience at its web site (e.g., a banner at the top of the page that says "Welcome back Joe").

by online users. But, by contrast, there is relatively little focus on protecting private information once it has reached its final destination. For example, many companies allow third parties to gain limited access to the information, but there is little or no discussion, and certainly no assurance that third parties won't further disseminate the information. Additionally, many online companies maintain consumers' private information on network servers that are directly connected to the Internet. This is typically done to enable information to be immediately recalled upon the customer's next visit to the site, thereby relieving consumers of the burden of constantly re-entering personal information every time they choose to make a purchase at the web site. Although this is an excellent time-saving consumer oriented feature, storing private customer information on a server attached to the Internet greatly increases the risk that someone will gain unauthorized access to that information.[3] Customers are therefore placed in the difficult position of either sharing private information and risking its unwarranted disclosure in order to conduct business online, refusing to provide the information and forgoing the transaction altogether or conducting it in a less convenient manner than desired.

The potential for losing control of one's personal information once it is released online is what prevents some people from engaging in Internet transactions. But some e-commerce industry observers believe this concern is overstated and contend that the potential nonconsensual transfer of personal information to third parties is not unlike what occurs in the mail order catalog industry. That is, when customers purchase items from mail order catalogs, there is a strong likelihood that their personal information will be forwarded to other catalog companies that sell similar or related items.[4] But, the primary difference between the catalog world and

---

3. Indeed, of late, it seems that hackers have turned their attention to breaking into secure servers attached to the Internet where they can gain access to massive amounts of private information. This is likely a more efficient process than randomly attempting to intercept private information as it travels across the Internet to its destination.
4. This process of sharing information with other mail order catalogs is analogous to the "profiling" done by online advertisers. That is, if a con-

the virtual world is that once personal information is transferred to a third party in the online environment, it costs very little for that third party to immediately begin contacting people and further distributing the information en masse. The bulk e-mail process allows online marketers to reach out and touch millions of people with a minimal investment of cost, time, and effort. In contrast, the real world marketing process must judiciously target consumers who are likely to purchase the items offered because of the significant costs that accompany typical mass market mailing campaigns. When suddenly bombarded with e-mail from individuals and companies marketing products in which they have no interest (commonly known as "unsolicited bulk e-mail"), consumers who value controlling their personal information are likely to feel very annoyed and perhaps even appalled at the complete invasion of privacy. Another factor that distinguishes e-mail mass marketing from real world bulk mailings is the relative ease and low cost of obtaining names and e-mail addresses. Thus, unscrupulous individuals may easily obtain private information, which not only increases the likelihood of receiving objectionable or obscene material, but also raises the specter of identity theft and other forms of fraudulent activity, depending upon the nature of the information acquired. The gaps in online policies that allow these potential privacy breaches suggest that further regulatory efforts are necessary to stimulate maximum compliance with basic privacy guidelines.

However, in furtherance of the self-regulation model, an alliance of 39 Internet companies and a dozen trade associations formed the Online Privacy Alliance (OPA). OPA's mission is to encourage the use of *posted* privacy polices and, in support of that goal, each member of the alliance agreed to adopt and implement a privacy policy. The OPA also utilizes third parties, such as the Better Business Bureau, TRUSTe, and WebTrust, to give web sites a "good seal of approval" if they are considered "privacy-friendly" sites. To obtain this seal of approval, web sites are required to meet

---

sumer regularly purchases merchandise from a high-end watch catalog, she might soon begin receiving catalogs from other mail order catalog companies selling high-end jewelry products.

four essential requirements. First, the sites must provide clear notice to visitors about their data collection and use practices. Next, the sites must obtain permission from consumers before using any collected data and also provide reasonable access to such data. Finally, web sites must take reasonable steps to protect the security of the information. The hope is that displaying the seal of approval on web sites will increase consumer confidence and confer a marketing advantage, thereby encouraging other online companies to seek the seal of approval by instituting and enforcing privacy guidelines.

Initiatives like the OPA indicate that the e-commerce industry has a strong interest in developing and enforcing strict privacy guidelines. Undoubtedly, this interest is driven, in part, by economic motives. That is, if the primary reason for consumer ambivalence regarding the Internet involves concerns about loss of control of private information, then these same consumers are less likely to frequent web sites that do not make a sincere effort to protect private information. This suggests that the online privacy issue is a two-fold educational process. First, those within the e-commerce industry must recognize the absolute necessity of implementing online privacy policies. Second, consumers must educate themselves about the hazards of various online activities and increase their overall awareness of web site privacy policies before choosing to entrust private information.

To aid this educational process, the Federal Trade Commission has convened several task forces of industry representatives and privacy and consumer advocates to develop strategies for more widespread implementation of privacy standards. The FTC also periodically holds a variety of workshops directed to both the business and consumer communities concerning online privacy. For instance, the FTC organized a public workshop addressing the topic of online profiling, which is the practice of aggregating information about consumers' preferences by tracking and gathering such information from their online activities. As one FTC report observed, the "Commission is committed to the goal of full implementation of effective protections for online privacy in a manner that promotes a flourishing online marketplace...."

In pursuit of the goal of full implementation, the FTC established an Advisory Committee on Online Access and Security to consider the equally important issues of access and security as they relate to online information. The committee's specific charge was to give advice and recommendations to the FTC concerning how best to provide online consumers with reasonable access to personal information collected from and about them by domestic commercial web sites, while also maintaining adequate security for that information. On the issue of access, the Advisory Committee proposed four different models or options for consumer access to private information.[5] The first option, which is described as the "Total Access Approach," declares that commercial web sites should provide access to all personal information regardless of medium, method, source of collection, or type of data in question. This option presumes that consumers have an absolute right to know what type of information is kept about them on any web site and to discover how the information is collected and used. This virtually unlimited access to information gives customers more control over their private information and may enable them to make better decisions as to how and when to disclose such information in an online environment. Critics caution, however, that unlimited access to information by consumers will be costly to online businesses from both a practical and technological standpoint. On the technology side, broad access to information will require businesses to obtain more powerful computer technology and increase human resources to handle the myriad access requests from consumers. From a practical perspective, if personal information is mistakenly released under a total access policy, the likelihood of greater harm to consumers exists because the open access policy permits access to *all types* of information collected and used by the web site. Consumers therefore face the potential of an even greater loss of privacy in the event of an erroneous release of their personal information.

Another option at the opposite end of the access spectrum suggests a limited release of information and is known as the "Access for

5. The four options are: total access approach, default to consumer access approach, case-by-case approach and access for correction approach.

Correction" approach. Under this option, consumers would have access to their information to challenge or correct errors if the web site uses that information to grant or deny a significant benefit to the consumer. Since there are fairly limited categories of information used to grant or deny benefits to consumers (e.g., credit reports and medical records), this policy would not cover information that is gathered for purposes of advertising and targeted marketing. Although this option enables consumers to correct information that impacts decisions made about them, it leaves untouched and inaccessible a wide range of information (such as aggregated advertising data) that may also be used unfairly and inappropriately.[6]

As noted above, the Advisory Committee report also addressed the separate but related issue of security of consumer personal information. This is the second part of a dual concern raised regarding the release of private information in an online environment, i.e., consumers want access to their personal information, but they also want to keep others from gaining unauthorized access to that information. Once again, the Advisory Committee developed a set of options for the FTC to consider in terms of defining parameters for the secure protection of online information.[7] The first option would rely upon existing legal and statutory remedies to serve as an incentive to web sites to adopt high information security standards. One of those existing legal remedies is litigation in the form of private tort actions against individuals or businesses for the improper release of private

---

6. To complete the discussion of the four access options, the default to consumer access approach means that personal information will not be accessible to consumers unless it can be retrieved by steps that the organization is capable of taking in the regular course of its business. This option seeks to ensure that businesses do not have to incur undue costs and burdens to provide access to personal information. The case-by-case approach, as the name suggests, would require analysis of different factors before information is accessible by consumers. These factors include, among other things, the content of the information, the holder of the information, the source of the information and the likely use of the information.

7. The five web site security options are: relying upon existing remedies, maintaining a security program, relying on industry-specific security standards, security standards that are appropriate under the circumstances, and a sliding scale of security standards.

information. According to some, the specter of litigation with its accompanying costs may be enough to encourage most online companies to adopt strict security guidelines. The downside of this approach, of course, is that the remedy is reactive in the sense that the consumer must wait for the harm to occur before seeking a remedy. Depending upon the nature of the harm, any damage recovery may be insufficient to redress the considerable injury that the consumer may have already suffered. A prime example of this is the Amy Boyer case discussed in the next section. Without question, an award of monetary damages in the Boyer case, no matter how high, will pale in comparison to the emotional pain and suffering that Amy's family endures as a result of her tragic murder.

Another security option proposes that an independent third party develop security standards for the online industry. This solution is the rough equivalent of the self-regulation model now used by the OPA and is appealing because security standards can then be customized to suit the specific needs of different sectors of the online industry. However, critics warn that without public accountability, self-regulatory organizations that are comprised solely of the industry at issue will not develop robust standards because doing so may subject its members to additional implementation costs and expose them to greater liability. But the larger question raised by this option is whether, under any circumstances, industry self-regulation provides the necessary security standards to not only maintain the confidence of those who are already online, but to also attract those who are hesitant to take part in the online experience for fear of losing control of their private information?

Dr. Larry Ponemon, a partner in PricewaterhouseCoopers and member of the Online Access & Security Advisory Committee, offers an intriguing normative access and security model designed to promote the long term success of e-commerce. Ponemon speaks about access and security as not simply fundamental principles by themselves, but "ways to engender transparency and stewardship by entities that collect, disseminate and profit from the use of personally identifiable information and other consumer-based data sources." Ponemon defines transparency as a process whereby good and bad players in the online environment are revealed *prior* to any exchange of information between the customer and the online entity. Stewardship, on the other hand, requires online entities to actively assume a fiduciary responsibility for the management and protection of private information entrusted to them. Ponemon posits that optimal conditions occur when transparency and stewardship for the online entity are both rated high. Under this scenario, consumers come to trust the online entity by virtue of its good actions, and therefore total access to personal information is not necessary to ensure privacy protection. However, when stewardship and transparency are rated low, then consumers will be extremely reluctant to trust online entities and maximum access to personal information will be required to encourage consumers to engage in Internet transactions.

Given this structure, Ponemon argues that it is incumbent upon online entities to devise ways to demonstrate and ensure trust. This includes providing appropriate notices and disclosures as well as establishing the equivalent of an online business ethos that zealously protects the privacy of consumer information. An online ethos that espouses transparency and stewardship holds the greatest potential for attracting reluctant consumers, particularly reluctant minority consumers, to the online environment. Fear and uncertainty in the areas of scientific and technological developments are likely to be based, in part, upon feelings that these processes are shrouded in mystery, which provides an optimum breeding ground for malicious, biased behavior. Transparent processes where "what you see is what you get" in online dealings and a stewardship approach where private information is protected by clearly enforced guidelines will inspire confidence in those who might otherwise avoid technology because of historically based fears and skepticism.

Privacy Regulation and Legislation

The Federal Trade Commission has broad investigatory and law enforcement authority over businesses engaged in or affecting commerce, which includes online businesses. Since 1995, the FTC has taken a proactive approach to educating the public about online privacy and examining web site practices regarding the collection, disclosure and use of private consumer information. Notably, when the FTC determined that web sites weren't doing enough to ensure that children's privacy was being protected as they surfed the Internet, it recommended that Congress enact legislation to protect minors. The Children's Online Privacy Protection Act of 1998 established guidelines for commercial web sites geared toward the protection of children's online privacy. These guidelines require operators of commercial web sites to, among other things, provide parents with notice of their information practices, obtain verifiable parental consent before collecting most personal information from children and maintain the security and confidentiality of the information they collect.

The FTC has also instituted legal action to protect consumers' online privacy. For example, when Reverseauction.com allegedly obtained consumers' private information from a competitor web site and sent unsolicited and deceptive e-mail to those customers, the FTC brought an enforcement action against the company. The charges were eventually settled, with Reverseauction.com agreeing to cease its marketing practices.

In addition to the FTC efforts, numerous Internet privacy bills were introduced into the 106th Congress. Ironically, observers generally agreed that these bills had little chance of passing given the Clinton administration's opposition to government regulation of online privacy. Nevertheless, several of the bills spoke squarely to the issue of online privacy and government regulation of web sites and online services. One example, the Online Privacy Protection Act, would require web sites and online services to provide individuals with notice of the types of personal information collected, how it is used, and how it is shared with others. Additionally, consumers would be given the opportunity to opt out of providing personal information for purposes other than those contained in the privacy notice. A similar bill, the Consumer Internet Privacy Protection Act, would regulate how interactive computer services treat private information. Specifically, these services could not disclose personally identifiable information without written consent of the consumer and would be required to provide consumers with copies of personal information maintained in their databases. Another bill, the Social

Security Online Privacy Protection Act, focuses on protecting consumers' social security numbers and other personally identifiable information from being distributed online. The Personal Data Privacy Act, which is perhaps the most extensive privacy bill in terms of potential entities subject to its regulation, would apply to businesses that collect personal data as well as local, state and federal government bodies. The bill contains a basic prohibition that "no Government agency or private entity may transfer, sell, or disclose any personal data[8] with respect to an individual to another Government agency or private entity without the express consent of the individual.[9]

Last, but certainly not least among these privacy measures, is a bill known as Amy Boyer's Law. This bill would significantly restrict access to social security numbers and was inspired by the tragic murder of twenty-year old Amy Boyer. In addition to this proposed legislation, the Boyer case sparked a first of its kind wrongful death lawsuit against Docusearch, a Florida company that provides detailed information about a person's life culled from public records, e.g., driving records, bank accounts, civil suits and property records. Indeed, Docusearch's motto is "This is the information age, and information is power! Discover the secrets of the people with whom you associate. Because what you don't know, can hurt you." According to the lawsuit, Liam Youens, a former high school classmate of Amy's, had become obsessed with her and created a web page on which he made threats to find Amy and kill her. Youens found the Docusearch web page and paid $204 for four searches designed to discover Amy's birthday, social security number, residence and place of employment. Once Youens learned where Amy worked, he stalked and killed her and then killed himself. The lawsuit, filed by Amy's family, seeks compensatory and punitive damages from Docusearch,

---

8. Personal data is defined broadly to include name, address, social security number, credit card information, Internet address, and medical or school information.

9. There is, however, an exception for governmental entities if the "transfer, sale or disclosure is for a national security purpose, law enforcement purpose or purpose relating to the Federal or State regulation of an industry."

alleging that Amy's murder could have been avoided if Docusearch had weeded out those requests that had the potential to lead to criminal acts. Although Docusearch expressly denies liability because it did not know of Youens' intentions and did not obtain Amy's personal information in an immoral or unethical manner, its web site no longer allows users to search for social security numbers.

Several bills address the increasingly controversial issue of governmental interception and collection of information from online communication sources. For instance, the Digital Privacy Act requires, among other things, reports by the FBI on its use of e-mail intercepts and blocks the use of electronic evidence in court if it is obtained illegally. Similarly, the Electronic Communications Privacy Act amends existing law to require annual reports to Congress on federal, state, and local agencies' monitoring of e-mail and other records.

As mentioned above, the FTC has also joined the call for online privacy legislation. In a May 2000 study, the FTC determined that only twenty percent of the busiest online sites implement all four fair information practice principles. As a result, the FTC reversed its previous position in favor of industry self-regulation and voted by a narrow 3–2 margin to call for legislation to "extend progress of self-regulation." In its report "Privacy Online: Fair Information Practices in the Electronic Marketplace," the FTC recommends that Congress enact legislation to ensure a minimal level of privacy protection for consumers. The Commission concluded that proposed legislation, in conjunction with self-regulation, will allow electronic commerce to reach its full potential and allow consumers to gain the confidence they need in order to participate fully in the electronic marketplace.

Although the Clinton administration has taken a government "hands-off"-industry self-regulation approach, the repeated demands for legislation from the FTC and other consumer and public interest groups has caused the administration to weaken its stance, particularly in light of lackluster industry participation in the self-regulation process. While the Administration still favors industry self-regulation, there have been hints that the federal government would be willing to step in should the industry's own efforts prove ineffective. Ironically though, it appears that the federal government can hardly claim the high ground in terms of privacy protection since it was recently discovered that very few government web sites actually adhere to the four fair information practices, even though most have privacy policies posted on their sites. Indeed, some of the more notable privacy breaches have originated from federal government web sites and agency actions. For instance, the practice of placing cookies on the computers of those who visited the Office of National Drug Policy Control and the FBI's "Carnivore" system mentioned above are a couple of the more recently disclosed examples.

Without a doubt, many black Americans still harbor fears about technology and its potential to invade privacy and inflict harm in covert ways. It is likely that these fears are exacerbated by daily reports of privacy violations, identity thefts and scams on the Internet. Of course, this is not to suggest that other groups are not also concerned about these Internet issues. Instead, it is to re-emphasize the unique historical viewpoint that blacks bring to the technology table. Reasonable, articulable and enforceable privacy standards, whether in the form of self-regulation or legislation or some combination thereof are a critical step toward securing the trust of black Americans and chipping away at the cynicism concerning science and technology that currently serves as a barrier to embracing the digital revolution.

Privacy Software

As technology helps online entities become more adept at collecting private information, software developers are scrambling to create consumer-friendly software designed to assist web surfers with maintaining control over private information while on the Internet. These "privacy promoting" software applications allow users to surf anonymously or with pseudonyms, filter material being transmitted to and from their computers and maintain control over their identities. Although there are a number of privacy software applications launched daily, government and industry officials are heavily touting the Platform for Privacy Preferences (P3P), a new protocol for sharing private information over the Internet. P3P assists web sites in developing online privacy statements that are comprehensible to the lay person, which enables consumers to clearly understand how their personal information is collected and shared. The technology also allows consumers to express privacy preferences through their web browsers and transmit those choices to web sites they visit. Those within the industry believe that web sites adopting privacy policies based upon the open and understandable P3P framework will greatly enhance consumer confidence because such policies contribute to the overall transparency of web sites embracing these standards. As discussed above, such transparency fosters a sense of consumer trust, which reduces the need to have complete access to information collected by the site.

The Cost of Technology

Chapter 2 described how historical economic disadvantage plays a considerable role in the inability of black Americans to afford computer technology, even at its currently reduced prices. When the choice is between buying groceries or getting a personal computer, there is really no choice at all. And even when black families have sufficient resources to purchase non-essential items, computers do not rank highly on their lists of acquisitions because computer technology simply doesn't seem relevant and may even pose a threat to personal privacy. While the question of relevance is largely one of education and is addressed elsewhere is this book, making technology economically feasible is still an essential component in the overall effort to narrow the digital divide.

In the current technology marketplace, personal computer manufacturers have begun to stake out the lower-price, first-time computer buyer as a target market, with the hope of securing a loyal customer base that will remain with the manufacturer's products when it's time for the inevitable upgrades. In addition, the introduction of the "Free PC" phenomenon has placed computers in the homes of those who might not otherwise be able to afford them. Under "Free

PC" programs, companies provide customers with free personal computers for a minimal monthly Internet access fee, which usually starts around twenty dollars a month. Of course, as the saying goes "there is no free lunch" and the free PC "catch" is that buyers must usually sign long term ownership and Internet access fee contracts, typically ranging from two-to-three years. However, in this age of rapidly changing technology, at the end of a three year contract term, the computer and means of accessing the Internet are likely to be completely outdated. Additionally, with some free or low-cost PC plans, the actual cost of the computer may ultimately be higher than advertised because the customer may be required to purchase a monitor separately or incur other costs such as long distance fees when accessing the Internet.

In a few noteworthy free PC cases, companies have generously offered free computers to needy schools in exchange for allowing the companies to gather marketing data from students. This unique partnership between the business industry and education was threatened, however, when federal lawmakers proposed legislation to require schools to get parental consent before collecting personal information from students and using it for commercial purposes. In these cases, the true cost of a "free" personal computer was a potential loss of privacy.[10]

Nevertheless, these methods of purchasing computers have made technology much easier to acquire because the buying process is very much like obtaining and maintaining a cell phone in the sense that, in some cases, the cost of the physical equipment is rolled into the monthly payments for service. Cell phone technology has reached nearly universal acceptance, with market penetration at practically every racial and socioeconomic level. This is probably due to the fact that cell phones are perceived as useful and relevant devices and are easy to acquire. Similarly, making personal computers and Internet access economically feasible is an important first step toward getting

---

10. In light of these privacy concerns, at least one company has notified schools that it can no longer profitably offer free PCs and has asked the schools to either begin paying for the technology or return it to the company.

technology into many more minority homes. Obviously, the other important component is an educational process that demonstrates the relevance of technology in terms of its present and future applications. Various methods to accomplish this important educational goal are the subject of the next chapter.

Chapter 8

Relevance and Access

No matter how reasonably priced personal computers are now or in the future, people will simply not embrace computer technology on a widespread basis until it is also shown to be relevant to their daily lives. The cellular telephone has reached near universal acceptance because people from all walks of life can appreciate the convenience of communication anytime and anywhere. Simply put, the relevance of cell phone technology is transparent to the average person. Computers, on the other hand, do not exhibit the same transparent relevance. They are often perceived as difficult to understand, expensive to acquire and maintain, a potential portal for unwarranted invasions of privacy, and an irrelevant nuisance. Given these perceptions, it is clear that narrowing the digital divide requires so much more than simply making computers widely available to underserved populations. Instead, solutions to the disparity in technology ownership and use must be multi-tiered, taking into account the historical issues of race that have played a significant role in the current inequalities. This Chapter will focus on one of the essential components of any program dedicated to narrowing the digital divide: determining what minority communities want in the area of computer technology and tailoring hardware, software and online content to meet those requirements. Does this mean completely altering the methods and processes already in place or alienating current technology users simply on the off chance that such modifications will increase minority participation in the digital revolution? Not necessarily.

In March 2000, The Children's Partnership (TCP), a national non-profit organization that, among other things, identifies new trends and emerging issues that will affect children, published *On-*

line Content for Low-Income and Underserved Americans: The Digital Divide's New Frontier.[1] The report examined a key element of the digital divide and concluded that it is as important to create useful content on the Internet—material and applications that serve the needs and interests of millions of low-income and underserved Internet users—as it is to provide computers and Internet connections. TCP's report further identified the *types* of content that are most likely to appeal to those who are low-income, live in rural communities, have limited education or are members of minority communities. These categories of relevant content include:

1. employment, education, business development and other information;

2. information that can be clearly understood by limited-literacy users;

3. information in multiple languages;

4. opportunities to create content and interact with it so that it is culturally appropriate.

The report also notes that these users primarily want local content rather than access to national or global information sources, which have become the hallmark of the Internet. For example, the report found that low-income and minority users want information focusing on their local communities, such as local job listings (particularly jobs requiring entry-level skills); local housing listings; and community information about neighborhood events, local schools and near-by destinations for family outings. In addition, these groups are interested in finding relevant information about local service organizations, such as day-care, after-school programs and activities at local churches.

The report determined that in order to facilitate discovery of this local content, people want a relatively easy on-ramp to the Internet. In the real world, when many individuals in underserved communities seek information, they typically rely upon family and friends as resources. This means that in order to encourage this population to rely upon the Internet for such information, the content must be rel-

---

1. The report is available at <http://www.childrenspartnership.org.>

evant *and* access to that information must be at least as user-friendly and logistically easy to find as the traditional "word-of-mouth" resources. Current search engine technology, which is often cumbersome to use and likely to produce irrelevant results, would almost certainly not create strong incentives for underserved users to substitute the Internet as an alternative to their real-world resources.

Given these content and ease-of-use requirements, TCP's report identified four content-related barriers between the content that people want and what is currently available online.

Lack of local information. This particularly affects the nearly 21 million Americans over age 18 whose annual income is less than $14,150 for a family of three.

Literacy barriers. The majority of information on the Internet is geared toward those with average to advanced literacy levels. Yet, approximately 22 percent of Americans do not function at these literacy levels.

Language barriers. Approximately thirty-two million Americans cannot take advantage of the benefits offered by the Internet because English is not their first language and about 87 percent of the Internet is in English.

Lack of cultural diversity. The Internet largely caters to middle-to-upscale white Americans, which serves as a cultural barrier to those who would like to participate in online ethnic communities and create content related to their cultural interests and practices.

In early 2000, the Clinton-Gore administration established an aggressive agenda to help close the digital divide by harnessing the powerful forces of private sector competition and rapid technological progress in pursuit of the goal of creating digital opportunity for all. Recognizing that providing access to the technology is only the first step, their agenda also focuses on ways to provide the relevant skills training to underserved communities and promote content and software applications that will help empower those communities. Specific provisions of the program include:

- Two billion dollars over ten years in new tax incentives to encourage private sector companies to donate computers to libraries and community technology centers, sponsor community technology centers and provide technology training for their workers.

- One hundred million dollars to create up to 1000 community technology centers in low-income urban and rural communities. It is anticipated that these centers will empower low-income communities in a variety of ways. For example, children will be able to improve their performance in school by gaining access to high-quality technology after school. Perhaps more important however, these children will learn to appreciate the value of technology and be able to prepare for the high-tech workplace by acquiring specific information technology skills and training. Additionally, adults can make use of the centers to obtain literacy training, employment search skills and realize entrepreneurial dreams.

- Fifty million dollars for a public/private partnership to expand home access to computers and the Internet for low-income families. Potential partners in this competitive grant program include high-tech companies willing to provide discounts on computers and access, local school districts seeking to expand parental involvement in education and libraries offering training in information literacy.

- Forty-five million dollars to promote innovative applications of information technology for underserved communities. These applications could include public health information systems, telementoring opportunities for at-risk youth, and communication and networking technology to enhance a sense of community.

These budget priorities reflect the fundamental notion that as we are increasingly becoming an information technology driven society, those without basic competencies in these areas will be relegated to a permanent underclass status. Thus, allocating funds to bring technology into underserved communities and homes is a definitive preemptive strike against a more permanently divided society.

Community-Based Efforts to Bridge the Digital Divide

Envision a room in a HUD-assisted and/or -insured housing development lined with computer workstations. Add a mix of people to make it work (residents, multifamily housing owners and managers, paid and volunteer staff, and community partners), plus a menu of educational and job training programs. Open the doors—both on-site and via the Internet—to microenterprise and telecommuting opportunities for residents. Introduce health care, wellness, community and social service programs. This is a Neighborhood Networks center tailormade to fit a local community.

—From the HUD web site

Because the reasons for lack of access to technology or apathy concerning technology education vary across communities, it is logical to craft solutions that focus on individual communities and develop specialized programs to meet the needs of those communities. The federal government has instituted a community-based approach in partnership with private corporations to develop some rather innovative programs to narrow the digital divide.

For example, the Housing and Urban Development agency (HUD) has created "network neighborhoods," a unique public/private partnership that establishes computer-based multi-service centers to help people in public and assisted housing learn the necessary computer skills to prepare for the technology job market. According to HUD, residents in HUD housing can utilize these community technology centers to enhance their computer literacy, launch new careers, make the transition from welfare to work, have expanded access to necessary health services, and participate in inter-generational learning activities. Importantly, HUD efforts have gained the recognition and support of community partners, such as local businesses, non-profit corporations, educational institutions, faith-based organizations, civic organizations, foundations, hospitals, community clinics, and federal and state government agencies. This predominantly local participation helps to ensure that HUD's efforts are indeed "community-based" rather than imposed from the outside. The program also emphasizes youth involvement and encourages children in low-income environments to pursue math and science careers, fields where minorities are traditionally underrepresented.

Because formulating solutions to close the digital divide is such a vital concern, the government is not content to keep its "tool kit" for bridging the digital divide under lock and key. Indeed, the Office of Educational Technology publishes the "Tool Kit for Bridging the Digital Divide in Your Community," for community leaders, government staff, business leaders and grass roots volunteers who want to cultivate community resources in an effort to narrow the gap in their local communities. While the tool kit doesn't guarantee success with any particular project, it does serve as a detailed roadmap for community technology program design from start to finish. The tool kit suggests that the first step toward developing programs that really help communities is gathering information about gaps that cause the digital divide. This information gathering process will aid in identifying the target population within the community, assessing its current technology skill level, and surveying what efforts are already being made to address the population's technology needs. The tool kit also emphasizes the need to build coalitions within the community, recognizing that often the best ideas fail at the community level because various constituencies feel left out of the planning process and, as a result, withdraw much needed financial or moral support. Therefore, inviting the various community coalitions to "sign-on" to the project at the beginning is not only an important initial step, but could ultimately determine the feasibility of the project.

The tool kit also recommends establishing realistic goals for community technology programs and developing benchmarks to determine whether those goals have been met. For example, if the goal is increased computer literacy, then a benchmark to measure progress toward that goal might establish that within a year there should be a fifty percent increase in the number of computer classes offered to the target population.

Last, but certainly not least, the tool kit suggests ideas for identifying resources for the project. Since this is probably the most important aspect of any community based plan and because resources are likely to be few and far between, the tool kit suggests being "creative" in seeking out those resources, but cautious in not allowing those who provide the resources to dictate the direction of the program. Examples of potential sources include individuals within the community, donations in kind, matching funds, government programs and non-profit organizations. Because some funds may be available in the form of grant money, the tool kit provides tips on how to write an effective grant proposal.

One concrete solution that may result from a community based effort to implement the guidelines in this tool kit is the creation of a community access center (CAC). Interestingly, CACs are not a modern concept and have been around since 1980, long before the Internet became a household name. They originated and continue to evolve from grassroots efforts to make computers, the Internet, software and technology training available to underserved communities. Evaluations of CACs in existence have demonstrated that they routinely serve much broader purposes than simply introducing individuals to technology. Indeed, most users leave the CAC experience with a much greater sense of accomplishment and self-confidence than when they entered because they are able to learn and, in some cases, master skills that they previously believed were unattainable.

CACs can be designed around a variety of models although most are non-profit and designed to serve the needs of a particular community. The Community Technology Centers' Network (CTCNet), a pioneer organization in the development of CACs, has identified four technology center models, which are classified according to their target populations and the level of services offered. First, there are the general-public-oriented technology centers, which are open to anyone in the community, and provide access to and training on computer, telecommunications and video technology. Next, the particular-populations-oriented centers, which target specific populations such as homeless or low-income families, and offer computer training as one component of an overall program to help people transition to self-sufficiency. The third type of center, known as a multiservice center, often provides a host of social services to needy families such as child care and after school programs. Computer access and training are simply additional services offered to this target population. Finally, the fourth model, community technology program networks, serves the dual purpose of offering computer access and training and assisting others to establish similar programs in separate areas of the community.

Of course, the specific technology programs and opportunities offered by CACs vary according to the target population and overall focus of the center. Most often, however, CACs offer either general public access to computer technology or formalized training in computer skills or a combination of the two. Typically, a CAC offering general public access allows anyone within the target population to use the center for purposes of developing computer skills or exploring various technology on an individualized basis. Computers and other technology equipment are usually available on a first-come, first served basis. In comparison, CACs offering formalized training programs generally provide a range of courses and seminars geared toward users at various skill levels and can accommodate those who merely want to become computer literate as well as those seeking specialized career training.

In keeping with its emphasis on community based solutions, HUD enthusiastically supports the creation of CACs. Indeed, to assist those specifically interested in establishing a CAC, HUD offers a sample business plan on its web site. According to HUD, the business plan is a "tool that allows Network Neighborhood planners to *think* through their ideas, solidify their intentions and objectives, and work efficiently with a plan towards specific goals." HUD acknowledges that individual network neighborhoods will be different depending upon their local constituencies, but suggests that planners follow a similar "first step" toward creating the network neighborhood. For instance, critical "rules of thumb" offered by HUD to fledgling network neighborhoods include: planning for self-sufficiency, budgeting for financial sustainability, encouraging residential involvement in planning, implementation and maintenance, establishing a plan for measuring successes and results, ensuring access to the Internet, and focusing on building local and federal partnerships. Although HUD plays a pivotal partnership role in helping to establish network neighborhoods, it is evident from this business plan template that as soon as practicable, network neighborhoods should endeavor to become financially independent while maintaining a focus on local involvement and partnership opportunities. On its web site HUD also includes links to potential funding sources to help network neighborhoods gain access to necessary finance programs and activities. These funding sources range from companies offering in-kind services and products to companies distributing up to $70 million dollars to support technology and literacy programs in urban and rural communities.

One rather unique approach to establishing CACs to bridge the digital divide involves the use of faith-based organizations as sponsors or developers of these community technology centers. Because the church often serves a central function in the everyday lives of black Americans, it is the one organization that is most apt to become intimately familiar with the life circumstances of individuals within the community. This extensive access to information within the community places the church in an unparalleled position to effectively assess the community's needs and structure programs to adequately address those needs. Churches can then take a "holistic approach" to resolving the digital divide. This means that not only can they institute programs that provide Internet access and computer literacy development, but they can also address some of the more systemic problems that contribute to the digital divide. For example, from a technology perspective, a faith-based CAC can provide literacy training, critical thinking skills development, and professional skills development to help prepare its constituents for the digital revolution. However, from a human perspective, the faith-based CAC is in a unique position to provide personal and financial counseling, health education, food, clothing and other forms of support that address and relieve some of the core socioeconomic issues that prevent people from actively participating in the digital revolution. In this way, churches can build upon their reputations of trust in the community as a means to draw people into technology oriented programs they may not otherwise feel comfortable with due to initial fear and skepticism and a lack of appreciation for the life-enhancing value that technology skills can provide.

One example of a faith-based CAC is the Neighborhood Learning Center in Washington, D.C. According to the Executive Director,

Julie Campbell, being a faith-based center allows the organization to utilize the gifts and talents of a large number of church volunteers who are committed to service. These volunteers give freely of their time and resources for purposes of training staff and maintaining, upgrading and donating computer equipment. Volunteers who work in the technology industry also serve as vital connections to technology companies that may agree to support the efforts of the CAC and provide equipment and other in-kind services to the organization. Finally, being a faith-based organization allows the Neighborhood Learning Center to forge partnerships with other organizations and foundations that value the faith-based community's holistic approach to providing educational support to its constituents.

Another innovative approach to developing community access centers involves organizing around a theme that focuses on a serious community issue such as health care for the elderly. As the HUD web site points out, "[t]he World Wide Web has become an important tool for seniors seeking information about health and health-related issues. Neighborhood Network centers, equipped with computers and Internet access, link these seniors with the kinds of relevant information that can keep them healthy and productive, regardless of their age." An example of this type of theme-based neighborhood network is the Golden West Neighborhood Network in Colorado, which allows senior citizens to research the safety of new medications, join online support groups, and consult with an online physician if necessary. In fact, the HUD web site boasts that the Golden West Neighborhood Network empowered a 77-year-old resident to utilize health related Internet resources to change her life. As the web site describes, the elderly Internet surfer obtained information that "helped her make informed decisions about changing her diabetes regimen, treating an Achilles tendon injury, and understanding the cause of heart palpitations. She also became more informed about standard medications and alternative remedies. As a result of her new knowledge, she and her physician can cooperatively plan and manage her health care."

These examples illustrate that the solution to the digital divide lies not in simply providing computers, but in also addressing fundamental issues that have served as barriers to the advancement of underserved communities. But just how effective are CACs at removing these obstacles and creating sustainable opportunities for targeted populations? In 1998, CTCNet conducted a survey designed to increase understanding of the impact of community technology centers, primarily in the areas of employment, learning, personal gains, and sense of community. The 817 survey participants ranged in age from 13 to 91 and were trained primarily at CACs that provided general access to computers and related technologies and targeted underserved or otherwise disadvantaged populations. Two-thirds of the study participants were from minority groups, with 37% identifying their background as "African descent." Thus, the study provides a unique glimpse into how effective CACs are, particularly when it comes to addressing the needs of minority communities.

The CTCNet survey measured the impact of CACs on increasing employment opportunities by asking survey participants if they had a job-related goal for using the technology center and, if so, how close they were to reaching that goal at the time of the survey. According to the results, most of the survey participants came to the center with job-related goals and over one-third of those responding indicated that they had reached or nearly reached their goals. More important, however, use of the Internet to search for employment prospects appeared to be a critical factor in determining whether job-seekers achieved their employment objectives or felt they were a lot closer to achieving them. That is, 60% of job seekers who sought employment on the Internet while at the CAC indicated that they were a lot closer or had reached their goals, while only 33% of non-Internet job seekers reported similar feelings about their employment searches.

The CTCNet study also discovered, among other things, that CACs are important factors in the self-development and upward mobility of their users. In particular, users felt comfortable learning at the centers and gained greater confidence in their abilities to master computer technology skills. With increased self-assurance, many users were able to fulfill personal, educational and employment objectives as they increased their competency with computer technology. Although many users obtained these tangible benefits from the centers, one of the more frequently mentioned comments revealed that CACs provide a significant intangible benefit by offering a comfortable, supportive learning atmosphere that fosters a sense of community, which, in turn, allows real community building to occur.

As the saying goes, "one of the first steps toward obtaining treatment for any problem is recognizing that indeed a problem exists." Similarly, one of the critical first steps toward closing the digital divide involves getting the target population to recognize the need for technology education and training. According to the CTCNet survey, this is, in fact, the greatest challenge for CACs, which often find that traditional advertising methods do not necessarily penetrate the target populations as much as desired. However, the survey discovered that word-of-mouth served as the method by which more than half of the survey participants discovered CACs. Specifically, people heard from a trusted relative or friend that they could obtain computer skills and training for little or no cost and decided to take advantage of the opportunity.

Although CAC participants sought to accomplish a variety of goals at the centers, such as furthering their education, improving computer skills and finding employment, most enjoyed the opportunity to take part in self-directed or self-motivated activities, such as using computer technology to edit a newsletter or pursue a personal hobby. The survey also revealed that once users became comfortable with the ins and outs of computers, their computer-related activities often branched out beyond simple word processing into Internet surfing and using e-mail. Some were so encouraged with their progress that they began to experiment further and developed familiarity with peripheral computer products such as scanners and printers.

Surprisingly, the survey revealed that a majority of CAC users had access to computers at home or at work yet still chose to utilize the centers as a resource for technology use and training. One reason offered for this overlap in usage was that centers typically provided better or more powerful computers and software applications. Many also preferred the centers because of their supportive learning environments coupled with the opportunities to communicate with other similarly situated individuals. This emphasis on the dynamic social aspects of CACs once again underscores the community building function of the centers. If, in fact, one of the barriers to embracing technology is skepticism and fear concerning its usefulness and potentially harmful effects, then finding a comfortable, encouraging environment that permits learning and interaction with other center participants and instructors will indeed be recognized as a vital function of CACs in the eyes of many participants.

In the final analysis, CACs are encouraging and enabling an otherwise underserved segment of our population to assume active roles in our technology oriented society. In light of previous studies that have demonstrated that underserved communities are either too fearful, too poor, too discouraged, or too disenfranchised to take more traditional paths to acquiring technology skills, CACs have distinguished themselves as one of the few avenues that the disenfranchised can take to becoming technologically literate.

In addition to periodic empirical studies of the impact of CACs, the HUD Neighborhood Networks Computer Learning Center Assessment and Evaluation provides an annual method for CACs to measure their own progress toward creating a technologically literate and productive society. The assessment form focuses on key criteria related to educational achievement and economic self-sufficiency. For example, network neighborhoods are encouraged to report whether and to what extent the center improved the academic achievement of school-aged children and increased adult education levels. On the economic front, the centers are asked to discuss how they reduced welfare dependency, expanded community based job training and encouraged small business ventures using the computer learning centers. The ultimate goal is to create a self-sustaining computer learning center that fosters an attitude of progress and self-sufficiency among its constituents.

The Future of Community Access Centers

Empirical studies and anecdotal evidence indicate that CACs are an important, relatively cost-effective solution to reach the greatest number of underserved individuals in low-income, minority communities. In fact, as the CTCNet study demonstrated, CACs have the greatest potential to narrow the digital divide because they aim to respond to and redress much of the historical baggage that plagues underserved communities and prevents them from actively participating in the digital revolution. For example, as discussed in Chapter 3, it is an undisputed fact that minority communities continue to lag behind in educational opportunities due to a persistent inequality in the allocation of resources to schools in low-income, predominantly minority neighborhoods. Although introducing computer technology into the curricula of classrooms in low-income communities will further the important goal of equal educational opportunity, CACs can play a crucial supportive role by providing access to computer technology and training during non-school hours to help reinforce skills acquired in the classroom. Thus, minority students are less likely to be educationally hampered by the fact that they may not have access to technology in their homes.

Furthermore, to the extent that the legacy of racism has resulted in the exclusion of minorities from employment opportunities, CACs serve as valuable resources for obtaining job skills and learning about employment opportunities. The CTCNet survey lends empirical support to this observation. Again, a full sixty-five percent of the survey participants took classes at technology centers to improve their job skills, while forty-three percent sought jobs using CAC resources and either reached their goals or were a lot closer to obtaining employment.

Finally, CACs offer an opportunity to learn in a supportive environment, which may go a long way toward combating fears and negativity associated with computer technology. In fact, eighty-two percent of the respondents ranked this as the top reason for utilizing a CAC, even when they had alternative means to access technology. In addition to the community building atmosphere, more than half the CAC users identified finding out about local events, local government and/or state and federal government as important reasons for using the center, an important finding that supports the notion of continuing the focus on creating relevant content for underserved communities.

Because CACs provide so much more than basic computer skills, their short and long-term benefits are not measurable by simply looking at the computer skills that participants acquire. Instead, to get the complete picture, one must consider the increased self-confidence, motivation and community building "side effects" that result from these community-based programs when measuring the overall impact of CACs. Indeed, the opportunity for community and sharing proved to be a critical, albeit intangible, component that brought many people to the CAC and encouraged them to stay and expand their horizons. The challenge for the future then is to build upon this manifest interest in community and sharing by encouraging CAC "graduates" to serve as ambassadors in the effort to spread the gospel about the digital age and persuade the more reluctant "have-nots" to explore the tremendous opportunities offered by CACs. To paraphrase the HUD philosophy on network neighborhoods: The premise is simple. Recognizing the emerging role of technology in society, computer skills open the door to economic freedom, while also creating stronger, healthier and safer communities.

Appendix

Because relevant content on the Internet is a major barrier that prevents black Americans from fully participating in the digital revolution, I thought it might be helpful to add some information concerning black or African American resources on the Internet. As I began drafting a list of those web sites, I was reminded of the true impact of technology. Because the Internet makes information so accessible, rather than providing a written list, which may be outdated by the printing of this book, I will simply direct interested readers to do exactly as I did: Find an Internet search engine and enter the terms "black American web sites" or "African American web sites" and you will be treated to numerous web sites (some good, some not so good) that contain content relevant to the black American experience.

Selected Bibliography

Birdsall, William F. "The Digital Divide in the Liberal State: A Canadian Perspective." *First Monday*, no. 5 (2000).

Caskey, John P. *Fringe Banking: Check-Cashing Outlets, Pawnshops, and the Poor*. New York: Russell Sage Foundation, 1994.

Chenault, Brittney G. "Developing Personal and Emotional Relationships Via Computer-Mediated Communication." *Computer-Mediated Communication Magazine* 5, no. 5 (May 1998).

Cook, Meghan E. "What Citizens Want From E-Government." Center for Technology in Government. 2000.

Cook, Philip J., and Jens Ludwig. "The Burden of "Acting White": Do Black Adolescents Disparage Academic Achievement?" In *The Black-White Test Score Gap*, edited by Christopher Jencks and Meredith Phillips, 375. Washington, D.C.: Brookings Institution Press, 1998.

Cox, Beth. "Crossing the Great Digital Divide." ECommerce Guide. December 12 2000.

Douglass, Frederick. *Narrative of the Life of Frederick Douglass, an American Slave*. New York: Signet, 1968.

Ferguson, Ronald F. "Teachers' Perceptions and Expectations and the Black-White Test Score Gap." In *The Black-White Test Score Gap*, edited by Christopher Jencks and Meredith Phillips, 273. Washington, D.C.: Brookings Institution Press, 1998.

Franklin, Raymond S. *Shadows of Race and Class*. Minneapolis, MN: University of Minnesota Press, 1991.

Greenman, Catherine. "E-Mail Mentoring." *New York Times* October 12, 2000.

Harmon, Amy. "How Race is Lived In America: A Limited Partnership." *New York Times* June 14, 2000.

Harreld, Heather. "Measuring E-GOV Value." *Federal Computer Week* August 28, 2000.

— "Tallying Intangibles." *Federal Computer Week* August 28, 2000.

Jones, James H. *Bad Blood: The Tuskegee Syphilis Experiment.* New York: The Free Press, 1993.

Krueger, Alan B. "Internet is Lowering the Cost of Advertising and Searching for Jobs." *NewYorkTimes.Com* July 19 2000.

Kuhn, Peter, and Mikal Skuterud. *Internet and Traditional Job Search Methods, 1994–1999,* April 24 2000.

Kujovich, Gil. "Equal Opportunity in Higher Education and the Black Public College: The Era of Separate But Equal." *Minnesota Law Review* 72 (1987): 29.

Lawson, Raneta J. "The Child Seated Next to Me: The Continuing Quest for Equal Educational Opportunity." *Thurgood Marshall Law Review* 16, no. 1 (1990): 35.

Lewis, David L. *W.E.B. DuBois: Biography of a Race,* 1993.

Margo, Robert A. *Race and Schooling in the South, 1880–1950.* Chicago: University of Chicago Press, 1990.

McDonald, Tim. "Study: Americans Turning to Net for Health Info." *E-Commerce Times* August 10 2000.

McGarvey, Robert. "ZDNet:Small Business:Connecting the E-Com Dots." *Entrepreneur Magazine* March 8, 2000.

Mensh, Elaine, and Harry Mensh. *The IQ Mythology: Class, Race, Gender and Inequality.* Carbondale, Illinois: Southern Illinois University Press, 1991.

Morris, Robert. *Reading, 'Riting, and Reconstruction: The Education of Freedmen in the South, 1861–1870.* Chicago: University of Chicago Press, 1976.

Myrdal, Gunnar. *An American Dilemma: The Negro Problem and Modern Democracy.* New York: Harper & Brothers, 1944.

Ogbu, John. "Opportunity Structure, Cultural Boundaries, and Literacy." In *Language, Literacy, and Culture: Issues of Society and Schooling*, edited by Judith Langer, 154, 1987.

Ogden, Mike. "Why Amazon Will Survive in the Net Jungle." *Austin Business Journal* December 25 2000.

Oliver, Melvin L., and Thomas M. Shapiro. *Black Wealth/White Wealth: A New Perspective on Racial Inequality*. New York, N.Y: Routledge, 1995.

Oubre, Claude. *Forty Acres and a Mule: The Freedmen's Bureau and Black Land Ownership*. Louisiana: Louisiana State University Press, 1978.

Pavis, Theta. "Online Journalism Review, Features: E-Government Presence Growing." *Online Journalism Review* August 15 2000.

Peterson, Robyn. "Researching Companies to Ensure Job Security." *Internet.Com* November 28, 2000.

Puma, Michael J., Duncan D. Chaplin, and Andreas D. Pape. *E-Rate and the Digital Divide: A Preliminary Analysis From the Integrated Studies of Educational Technology*. The Urban Institute. 2000.

Raspberry, William. "Why is Busing the Only Route?" *Washington Post* September 4 1981, 29.

Regan, Keith. "The Name-Your-Problem E-Tailer." *E-Commerce Times* December 11 2000.

Rheingold, Howard. *The Virtual Community: Homesteading on the Electronic Frontier*. Reading, Mass.: Addison-Wesley, 1993.

Rowan, Carl T. *Dream Makers, Dream Breakers: The World of Justice Thurgood Marshall*. Little, Brown & Company, 1993.

Stampp, Kenneth M. *The Peculiar Institution*. New York: Vintage Books, 1989.

Steele, Claude M., and Joshua Aronson. "Stereotype Threat and the Test Performance of Academically Successful African Americans." In *The Black-White Test Score Gap*, edited by Christopher Jencks and Meredith Phillips, 401. Washington, D.C.: Brookings Institution Press, 1998.

Steinert-Threlkeld, Tom. "ZDNet: Business and Tech E-Commerce: GroceryWorks: The Low-Touch Alternative." January 31, 2000.

Stepanek, Marcia. "A Small Town Reveals America's Digital Divide." *BusinessWeek Online* October 4 1999.

Stites, Janet. "Prospectus: Black Entrepreneurs Spread the Word About "Digital Freedom"." *New York Times* [New York] February 22 1999.

Strangelove, Michael. "The Internet, Electric Gaia and the Rise of the Uncensored Self." *Computer-Mediated Communication Magazine* 1, no. 5 (September 1 1994).

Strenio, Jr., Andrew J. *The Testing Trap*. New York: Rawson, Wade, 1981.

Symonds, Matthew. "The Next Revolution." *The Economist* June 24 2000.

— "No Gain Without Pain." *The Economist* June 24 2000.

Turkle, Sherry. *Life on the Screen: Identity in the Age of the Internet*. London: Phoenix Orion Books, 1997.

Turner, Patricia A. *I Heard It Through the Grapevine*. Berkeley and Los Angeles: University of California Press, 1993.

Varianini, Vittoria, and Diana Vaturi. "Marketing Lessons from E-Failures." *The McKinsey Quarterly* 4 (2000).

Venezia, Todd. "Online Lover Accused of Scamming Women." *APBNews.Com* December 9 1998.

— "Online Relationship Ends in Death." *APBNews.Com* February 2 1999.

Web-based Education Commission. *The Power of the Internet for Learning: Moving From Promise to Practice*, December 21 2000.

Wright, Gavin. *Old South, New South: Revolutions in the Southern Economy Since the Civil War*. New York: Basic Books, 1986.

Zyskowski, John. "Harnessing the Internet Economy." *Federal Computer Week* 28/8 2000.

Index